ONE-DISH
STOVETOP MEALS

JANE MARSH DIECKMANN

THE CROSSING PRESS SPECIALTY COOKBOOKS

THE CROSSING PRESS **FREEDOM, CALIFORNIA**

For information on bulk purchases or group discounts for this and other Crossing Press titles, please contact our Special Sales Manager at 800-777-1048.

Visit our Website on the Internet at: www.crossingpress.com

Library of Congress Cataloging-in-Publication Data

Dieckmann, Jane M.
    One-dish stove top meals / Jane Marsh Dieckmann.
        p. cm. -- (Specialty cookbooks)
    ISBN 0-89594-968-7 (pbk.)
    1. Entrées (Cookery) 2. Stews. 3. Stir frying. I. Title.
  II. Series: Crossing Press specialty cookbooks.
  TX740.D52   1998
  641.8'2--dc21   98-26028
                              CIP

CONTENTS

This book is dedicated to you who are interested in wholesome food from different traditions, and especially to Inge and Walter, who represent the international at its very best.

INTRODUCTION

My philosophy in the kitchen is to keep dinner easy to make and tasty and healthful to eat. The recipes given here generally contain the principal elements of a meal, usually cooked in one pot or skillet on top of the stove. In many cases, the meal can be served right out of the pan. The addition of a salad or simple side dish, hearty bread, and a beverage completes the meal. My emphasis is on simplicity of preparation, the combination of fresh wholesome ingredients, and the borrowing of old and new ideas from cooking traditions worldwide.

Some Thoughts on Healthy Eating Today

The past ten years have seen many changes in attitudes concerning the best ways to select, prepare, and cook our daily meals. We are bombarded with bewildering concerns about food safety, good ingredient balance, and, especially, low-fat cooking. From my point of few, the major rules are simple: We should all eat a variety of foods, keep a healthy weight, and choose a diet that is low in cholesterol and fat, especially saturated fat. We should eat plenty of vegetables, grain products, and fruits. We should use only moderate amounts of salt, sodium products, and sugar. The dietary guidelines for lower cancer risk, for example, suggest a limited consumption of cured and smoked products; a greater proportion of fiber-rich and unrefined foods; and the inclusion of more vitamin- and beta-carotene-rich vegetables, such as broccoli, chard, peppers, spinach, carrots, sweet potatoes, and winter squash.

Here are the basics to understanding the issues of cholesterol and "good" fats versus "bad" fats—issues that confuse even the most well-informed people. Not all fats clog arteries and not all fats contain cholesterol, a substance that accumulates in deposits in the arteries, eventually restricting blood flow to the heart. Cholesterol is found in meat (especially red meat), egg yolks, and such dairy products as butter, cream, cheese, and whole milk. Saturated fats—so called because they are "saturated" with hydrogen—increase the risk of heart disease; eating them raises blood levels of cholesterol.

We should avoid tropical oils, such as coconut and palm oil, and cut down drastically on butter, cheese (especially cheese with a high fat content), whole eggs, and red meat. In a wholesome diet these foods would be replaced by more grains, fruits, vegetables, fish, and poultry, and such dairy products as skim milk, low- or reduced-fat cheeses, and low-fat or nonfat yogurt. Keep in mind that grains, legumes, fresh vegetables, and fruits contain no cholesterol at all, and most contain no fat at all, the notable exceptions being peanuts, soybeans, and avocados.

Although the jury is still out on many questions concerning fats and the ways our bodies use them, medical researchers agree that monounsaturated oils—olive oil, peanut oil, and canola oil—represent a better health bet than polyunsaturated oils—corn oil, soybean oil, safflower oil, and other vegetable oils. Of the monounsaturated oils, canola oil has the lowest amount of saturated fat. The best health bet is to cut down on fat altogether, regardless of whether it is saturated, polyunsaturated, or monounsaturated.

Seasoning

Try to use less salt and fewer seasonings with additives in your cooking. To my taste, some freshly squeezed lemon juice on lightly cooked fresh green beans tastes better than butter and salt.

Whenever possible, make your own meat, chicken, and vegetable stocks (see pages 11–13 for recipes and hints). If you must use commercial stocks, purchase the low-sodium varieties that contain the fewest additives.

Avoid salted and smoked meat products, and use low-sodium versions of condiments and flavorings, such as soy sauce, hot sauce, and salad dressing.

Remember to season judiciously. You can never take out what has been added, but you can always add more. Remember too that seasoning with herbs and spices often compensates for using less salt, which is, as we know, a healthy aim.

Use fresh herbs whenever possible, remembering that you need a greater quantity of fresh than dried herbs (about three times more) because the flavor is not so concentrated. Before adding fresh herbs, either mince them finely or rub the herbs between your fingers to release the flavors.

Basic Ingredients

Meat

The general rule for meat is to use much smaller amounts. Purchase the leaner cuts (they are often less expensive anyway) and trim off any visible fat. Purchase the leanest ground beef you can find, or buy a lean cut and grind it yourself. Avoid ground pork and lamb unless you can have it ground for you personally from very lean cuts. Many cooks use ground turkey or—for a high-protein, vegetable alternative—ground cooked soybeans, or textured vegetable protein.

Poultry

White-meat chicken and turkey are relatively low in fat, especially if you don't eat the skin. Turkey is leaner than chicken. The consensus among researchers is that removing the skin before cooking poultry will dry out the meat considerably, whereas leaving the skin on does not add noticeable fat to the dish, provided you remove the skin before eating.

Seafood

As a general rule, eat a variety of seafood and in moderation. Fish highest in omega-3 oils, which some doctors believe to be helpful in preventing blood clots, are salmon, mackerel, herring, and sardines; trout contains a smaller amount.

Shellfish that are stationary on the ocean floor—including clams, mussels, oysters, and scallops—contain only a small amount of cholesterol. Crustaceans that are mobile—crabs, crayfish, shrimp, and lobsters—contain some cholesterol but are quite low in saturated fat, shrimp containing the most.

Vegetables

Recent research points to the benefits of the dark green and orange vegetables and to the beta-carotene they contain, which is believed to protect against cancer. Why not include in your diet such orange and yellow vegetables and fruits as carrots, sweet potatoes, winter squash, pumpkin, mangoes, cantaloupe, and apricots, and such green vegetables as kale, spinach, broccoli, Swiss chard, and green bell peppers?

The taste and nutritional value of summer vegetables are highest with freshly picked produce. Winter vegetables store well and can be used anytime. Potatoes are an important part of the wholesome diet; they contain very little fat and are a good source of vitamin C, the B vitamins, and potassium. Scrub them well and there's no need to peel them.

Legumes

A staple food in most cuisines all over the world, legumes are economical, easily prepared, and brimming with nutrition in the form of protein, complex carbohydrates, vitamins, and minerals. There are many kinds of legumes, including soybeans, which contain more protein than any of the others.

The best way to serve legumes is to combine them with grains, providing "complete" protein with no cholesterol and very little fat. If you must use canned beans, be sure to rinse and drain them well.

And don't neglect the miraculous soybean products—tofu and tempeh. For most combination dishes firm tofu is the best. My favorite tempeh is the three-grain (millet, brown rice, barley) variety.

Grains and Pasta

In addition to rice, we have barley, bulgur, millet, and quinoa, not to mention grain by-products such as grain flours, rolled grains, cornmeal, and wheat germ—truly an endless bounty.

Long-grain and short-grain rice as well as basmati and texmati rice are sold in brown and white versions. Brown rice retains its outer bran and its germ, and hence has more vitamins and minerals than plain milled rice. White rice, however, if enriched, can have more nutrients than the natural brown rice product. All rice is a good source of B vitamins. The most nutritious way to serve rice is with legumes, since the combination produces complete protein.

Barley comes in two forms. Removing the husk results in pearl barley, which cooks more quickly but is lower in nutrients and fiber than whole barley. Whole barley can be presoaked for several hours before cooking, thus cutting down on preparation time.

Bulgur—the preferred grain of central Europe and the Middle East—is made by first boiling, then drying and grinding whole wheat. It is most readily available in a fine and a course grind. Cooking time is about 20 minutes, but when you make tabouli, you don't have to cook the bulgur at all.

Millet is a quick-cooking grain with a little crunch. Quinoa, which looks like it, is certainly worth a try. The best grade has a nutty, almost sweet flavor. Rinse under cold running water and drain. Combine it with heated liquid only and simmer it for about 15 minutes.

Pasta basically consists of water plus flour and/or semolina (the coarsely milled inner part of the wheat kernel, called the endosperm—the more semolina the pasta contains, the more protein it has). In addition to the most common forms, pasta comes made of whole wheat flour and in a high-protein form fortified with soy flour. Egg noodles, as their name indicates, are made with flour and water plus eggs. Couscous is coarsely ground semolina mixed into a dough and then rolled into tiny balls. For an authentic cooking method, see page 100.

Dairy Products

The following can help you to cook lean with cheese: Cheeses very high in fat (70 percent or more of the calories being derived from fat) are American, blue, Camembert, Cheddar, colby, cream cheese, feta, Muenster, Neufchâtel, and Parmesan. Cheeses moderately high in fat (50 to 70 percent of calories) include provolone, ricotta (both whole milk and part-skim, the latter having a lower percentage of fat), Romano, and mozzarella. Cheeses with a low fat content (20 to 35 percent of calories) are cottage cheese (regular and low-fat), pot cheese, and farmer cheese. (Cottage cheese is also available in a nonfat version, which has good flavor and texture.)

For lean cooking, use smaller quantities of whatever cheese you select. When making sauces and toppings, use grated rather than sliced cheese. This results in using less overall but with a barely noticeable difference in flavor.

As for milk, whenever possible use skim milk or canned evaporated skimmed milk. Nonfat dry milk can often be stirred into dishes to boost protein and calcium without adding any fat. Avoid cream of all kinds, as well as whole milk, even 2 percent milk, which seems low in fat but really isn't.

A Final Bit of Philosophy

This book presents appealing, comfortable food from various cooking traditions, prepared in an easy-going and uncomplicated way that reflects our need for a less frantic pace in the kitchen—all with the understanding that both our time and the quality of our lives are important.

The approach here is experimental and adventuresome. It encourages you to try various interesting and often unusual and unfamiliar combinations, adapting the best and most fruitful ideas to your own individual cooking and using what works well for you.

Cooking should be fun and relaxed; a meal should be enjoyed by everyone—including the cook—and consumed in a leisurely fashion. With good planning and ideas like those in this book, you should have time to sit down and relax before dinner, enjoy a conversation with the family, read the paper, and be ready to appreciate the good meal coming up. On the other hand, if you have worked all day, are starving, and want your meal quickly, most of the skillet recipes here can appear on your table, completely ready, within thirty minutes. Some dishes are even faster. Consult the index under quick recipes and versions.

Although I have made much ado about cooking wholesome, everyday meals for the whole family to enjoy, most dishes here can be served at a dinner party with pride. These meals are healthful and nutritious, delicious, and—above all—interesting. So in whatever language you want to say it and in whatever tradition you want to cook it, enjoy what follows and know that you are eating to your good health.

Stocks

The secret of good stock lies in fresh ingredients and sufficient cooking time. Try to make a considerable amount of stock at one time. Chill all stock before you use it and remove any fat that has risen to the top.

Homemade stock is perishable, although beef and vegetable stock will keep longer (up to a week) in the refrigerator than chicken and turkey stock (2 to 3 days).

If you want to keep the stock longer, store it in the freezer, where it will keep for at least 6 months. For safety's sake, before using stock—whether refrigerated or frozen—bring it to a full boil.

If you use canned stock, either as a supplement or as an ingredient in a recipe, remember that it is salted, so season accordingly.

Beef Stock

Remove all visible fat from 4 pounds raw beef bones, including some veal bones if you can get them, and some meat (include a piece or two of shin bone, if you like). Brown them in a wide soup pot over medium-high heat, or bake them, uncovered, in a 450°F oven until brown (about 30 minutes), turning once. Add 3 large onions, chopped, and brown them for part of the time. Let the pot cool somewhat and add 14 cups water, scraping the bottom of the pot to deglaze. Then add 4 medium carrots, coarsely chopped; 4 stalks celery, with tops, chopped; 3 cloves garlic, cut into pieces; 6 sprigs parsley; 2 bay leaves; 10 peppercorns; 2 teaspoons salt; and 2 tablespoons red wine vinegar. Bring the stock to a boil; then reduce the heat to low and simmer, partially covered, for 3 hours. Stir in 2 more tablespoons red wine vinegar and continue to simmer, partially covered, until the liquid is reduced to about 2 quarts. Strain. Use the meat and vegetables for soup, if you like. Makes 2 quarts.

Chicken Stock

If you have a chicken carcass from a roast, brown the bones in a wide stockpot over medium-high heat. Otherwise, boil 4 pounds chicken pieces (backs, necks, and wings) in 4 quarts water for 1/2 hour. Skim, then add 2 medium onions, quartered; 2 cloves garlic, quartered; 2 medium carrots, chopped; 2 stalks celery, with tops, chopped; 8 sprigs parsley; 10 peppercorns; 1 teaspoon salt; 1 teaspoon fresh thyme (or 1/2 teaspoon dried thyme); 1 tablespoon cider vinegar; and enough water to cover the chicken by 3 inches. Return to a boil; then reduce the heat to low and simmer, partially covered, skimming occasionally, until the stock is reduced to 3 quarts (about 3 hours). Strain. Makes 3 quarts.

Turkey Stock

I always save the carcass from the holiday roast turkey to make stock. Otherwise, you can use 4 pounds turkey pieces (backs, necks, and wings). In either case, follow the directions above for Chicken Stock, adding 1 teaspoon rubbed dried sage and 1/2 teaspoon dried rosemary to the stock.

Fish Stock

In a large stockpot combine 2 1/2 pounds heads and bones of firm-fleshed white fish, cleaned of blood and cut into 2-inch pieces, with 6 cups water and 1 cup dry white wine. Add 2 medium onions, chopped; 2 medium stalks celery, with tops, chopped; 6 sprigs parsley; 1 bay leaf; 8 peppercorns; 1 teaspoon salt; and the juice of 1 lemon. Bring to a boil, then reduce the heat to medium-low and simmer, partially covered, for about 1 hour. Strain. Makes 1 1/2 to 2 quarts. If you like, add 3 cups clam juice to the stock with the other ingredients.

Microwave version. Use 2 pounds fish heads and bones, 1 onion, 1 celery stalk, 1 carrot cut into 1-inch lengths, the seasonings given above, and 5 cups liquid. Place everything in a 2-quart soufflé dish, cover tightly with microwave plastic wrap, and cook on high (100%) for 20 minutes. Remove from the microwave and leave covered until the bubbling stops (about 3 minutes). Uncover carefully and strain.

Vegetable Stock

In a large stockpot combine 2 cloves garlic, cut; 5 medium onions, chopped; 4 stalks celery, with leaves, coarsely chopped; 1 bunch parsley; 1 teaspoon fresh lemon thyme or 1/2 teaspoon dried thyme; 1/4 teaspoon crumbled dried sage; 1 bay leaf; 1 teaspoon salt; 10 peppercorns, lightly crushed; 5 allspice berries, lightly crushed; and 4 quarts water. Bring to a boil; then reduce the heat to low and simmer, partially covered, until the liquid is reduced to about 2 1/2 quarts (about 2 hours). Stir in 1 tablespoon red wine vinegar and continue to simmer, uncovered, for 30 minutes longer. Strain, gently pressing the liquid out of the vegetables with the back of a spoon. Makes about 2 1/2 quarts.

To make Vegetable Stock with tomatoes, add 2 medium tomatoes, coarsely chopped, to the pot with the other vegetables.

Microwave variation. Combine the above ingredients, using only 3 quarts water, in a 5-quart casserole. Cover tightly with microwave plastic wrap and cook on high (100%) for 35 minutes. Prick the plastic wrap to release the steam; then remove from the oven and allow the stock to stop bubbling. Remove the cover. Strain, pressing to extract all the stock.

Root Vegetable Stock

In a wide stockpot over medium heat, warm 1 tablespoon canola oil. Stir in 3 large carrots;

chopped; 1 large turnip, chopped; 2 large stalks celery, with tops, coarsely chopped; 2 large onions, chopped; and 2 cloves garlic, quartered. Sauté the vegetables, stirring occasionally, until golden (about 15 minutes). Carefully pour in 3 quarts water, stir well, and add 1 teaspoon salt, 6 large sprigs parsley, 1 bay leaf, 1 teaspoon dried thyme, and 6 black peppercorns. Bring to a boil; then reduce the heat and simmer, partially covered, for about 2 hours. Strain, pressing on the strainer to extract all the liquid, and discard the vegetables. Makes about 10 cups.

Tomatoes

Tomato Sauce

In a large saucepan over medium heat, warm 1 tablespoon olive oil. Add 1 large onion, chopped; 1/2 green bell pepper, seeded and chopped; 2 stalks celery, with tops, chopped; 2 carrots, cut into pieces; and 1 large clove garlic, chopped. Sauté the vegetables for about 5 minutes. Then stir in 6 large tomatoes, quartered (or 4 cups canned tomatoes—reserve the juice for another use), 1 bay leaf, 1 teaspoon brown sugar, 3 sprigs parsley, 1 teaspoon dried basil, 1 teaspoon salt, and 1/4 teaspoon freshly ground black pepper. Reduce the heat to low and gently cook the sauce until thick (about 45 minutes), stirring occasionally. If the tomatoes are watery, drain off some of the juice and reserve for another use; it makes a lovely base for salad dressings or as a light vegetable stock for cooking rice or meat loaf. Discard the bay leaf and purée the sauce in the food processor. Makes about 4 cups.

You can also add 2 tablespoons dry red wine for a more robust flavor.

Microwave version. Place the onion, bell pepper, and garlic in a food processor and process until finely chopped. Heat the oil in a 2-quart soufflé dish, uncovered, on high (100%) for 1 minute. Stir in the chopped vegetables. Cook, uncovered, on high for 8 minutes, stirring once. Stir in the remaining ingredients and cook on high for 8 minutes. Taste and adjust the seasonings.

Crushed Tomatoes

This is a quickly made microwave concentrate for use in sauces and soups or as a salad dressing base. Freeze it in 1-cup and 2-cup portions and also in an ice cube tray to add quick tomato flavor to a dish.

Remove the core and cut a deep X across the bottom of 12 medium tomatoes. Place in a 2 1/2-quart soufflé dish or square baking dish. Cook, uncovered, on high (100%) for 20 minutes, stirring once. Remove from the microwave and pass through a food mill. You should have about 8 cups cooked tomatoes.

Return them to the dish. Cook, uncovered, on high until all the liquid has evaporated (about 45 minutes). Remove from the oven and let cool completely. Store, tightly covered, in the refrigerator, or freeze as indicated above. Makes about 4 cups.

Tomato Purée

Combine 5 pounds plum tomatoes, cored and cut into 1-inch pieces, with 12 cloves garlic, mashed, in a 4-quart saucepan. Stir in 1/4 cup olive oil. Simmer, uncovered, stirring occasionally, until the tomatoes and garlic are soft (about 1 hour). Pass the mixture through a food mill or sieve, discard the pulp, and return the purée to the pan. Simmer, uncovered and stirring often, until the mixture becomes thick (1 to 1 1/2 hours). Cooking time depends considerably on the tomatoes used. Stir in 1/2 teaspoon salt and 1/2 teaspoon freshly ground black pepper. Taste and add more seasoning, if desired. Store, tightly covered, in the refrigerator for up to 1 week or freeze for up to 2 months. Makes 4 cups.

Microwave version. Combine the tomatoes, garlic, and oil in a 5-quart casserole dish with a tight fitting lid. Cover and cook on high (100%) for 15 minutes. While the dish is still in the microwave, uncover and stir, then cover and cook until the tomatoes and garlic are soft (about 10 minutes longer). Purée as above, then return the dish to the oven. Cook, uncovered, on high, stirring occasionally, until the mixture becomes thick (35 to 45 minutes). Season to taste.

Sauces and Dressings

Hot Pepper Sauce

In a small saucepan combine 1/4 cup olive oil, 2 1/2 teaspoons cayenne pepper, 1 1/2 teaspoons cumin, 1 clove garlic (crushed in a press), and 1/4 teaspoon salt. Cook until well blended. Serve warm. Good over fish dishes and stews.

Sesame Dressing

In a 2-cup measure combine 4 tablespoons water, 2 tablespoons rice vinegar, 2 tablespoons low-sodium soy sauce, 1 tablespoon Asian sesame oil, 1/4 teaspoon Chinese five-spice powder, and 1 tablespoon sesame seeds, toasted. Makes more than 1/2 cup.

Light Herb Dressing

Combine 1/2 cup Vegetable Stock (page 12) or thin tomato juice with 1/4 cup red wine vinegar, 1/4 teaspoon Italian Herb Blend (page 16), 1 small clove garlic (crushed in garlic press), and a dash freshly ground black pepper. Makes a little more than 3/4 cup.

Creamy Orange Dressing

In a blender combine 1 cup nonfat cottage cheese, 1/2 cup orange juice, 1 tablespoon honey, 2 teaspoons grated orange zest, 1 teaspoon ground mustard, and a dash salt. Process at high speed until smooth. Makes about 1 cup.

Pesto

In a food processor combine 4 cups fresh basil leaves, 3 cloves garlic, chopped coarsely; 1/2 cup pine nuts, 1/2 cup flat-leaf (Italian) parsley, 1/4 cup olive oil, and 1/4 teaspoon salt. Blend to a smooth paste. If it is too thick, add a little water. Then add 1/4 cup Parmesan cheese and process again. To use as a sauce over pasta, dilute with 2 tablespoons of the hot pasta water and toss with the cooked pasta.

Marinade for Vegetables

In a food processor chop 1 onion, 2 shallots, 1/2 carrot, 1/2 celery stalk, with tops, and 1 clove garlic. In a large saucepan heat 1/4 cup olive oil; sauté the chopped vegetables until soft and lightly browned. Stir in 3/4 cup cider vinegar or white wine vinegar, 2 cups light red wine, 1 bay leaf, 1 teaspoon dried thyme, 1/2 teaspoon ground coriander, 1/2 teaspoon salt, and 1/2 teaspoon freshly ground black pepper. Simmer, uncovered, for about 40 minutes. Discard the bay leaf. Let cook completely. Use as a dressing over warm slightly cooked vegetables. Makes about 3 cups.

Microwave version. In a 2-quart soufflé dish, heat the oil on high (100%) for 1 minute. Add the chopped vegetables and cook, uncovered, on high for 8 minutes, stirring once. Add the remaining ingredients, stir, and cook on high for 10 minutes, stirring once or twice. Let cool and discard the bay leaf.

Yogurt Cheese

Line a strainer or colander with a damp cheesecloth about 20 inches square. Pour in 4 cups plain nonfat yogurt. Fold the cloth over and twist the ends to form a pouch. Place the pouch over a large bowl and let it drain at room temperature for 3 to 5 hours, then refrigerate until the next day. Discard the liquid. Unwrap and invert the yogurt cheese onto a serving plate. Store, covered, in the refrigerator. Use in cooking or blend with herbs for a dip or spread.

Herbs and Seasonings

Italian Herb Blend

You can buy commercial Italian seasoning or you can make your own by combining 3 tablespoons dried oregano, 2 tablespoons dried basil, 1 tablespoon dried marjoram, 1 tablespoon dried thyme, and 2 teaspoons crushed dried rosemary in a 4-cup measure. Blend and crush somewhat with your fingers. Store in an airtight container in a cool, dry, dark place. Makes about 1/2 cup.

Herbes de Provence

Combine the following herbs: 3 tablespoons dried thyme, 3 tablespoons dried marjoram, 2 tablespoons dried summer savory, 1 teaspoon dried rosemary, 1 teaspoon crumbled dried mint, 1/2 teaspoon fennel seeds, 1/4 teaspoon rubbed dried sage, and 1/4 teaspoon dried lavender flowers. Store in a jar with a tight-fitting lid.

Crush with a mortar and pestle before using. Makes about 1/2 cup.

Cajun Pepper Mix

Combine 2 tablespoons paprika, 4 teaspoons cayenne pepper, 2 teaspoons coarsely ground black pepper, 1 teaspoon dried chives, 1 teaspoon dried basil, 1/2 teaspoon freshly ground white pepper, 1/2 teaspoon crushed red pepper flakes, 1/4 teaspoon onion powder, and 1/4 teaspoon garlic granules. Mix together thoroughly. Store in an airtight container in a cool, dry, dark place. Makes about 1/3 cup.

Dumplings and Quick Breads

Parsley Dumplings

In a medium bowl combine 1 cup all-purpose flour, 2 teaspoons baking powder, 1/4 teaspoon salt, 2 teaspoons canola oil, 3 tablespoons minced parsley, and 1/2 cup skim milk until just moist.

Note: To make cornmeal dumplings, substitute 1/4 cup yellow cornmeal for 1/4 cup of the flour and increase the liquid slightly.

Skinny Corn Bread

In a medium bowl combine 3/4 cup yellow cornmeal, 1/2 cup whole wheat flour, 2 teaspoons baking powder, 1/2 teaspoon baking soda, and 1/4 teaspoon salt. In a 4-cup measure combine 1 beaten egg, 1 tablespoon honey, and 3/4 cup skim milk or buttermilk; pour over the cornmeal mixture, stirring until just moistened. Pour into a lightly oiled 9- by 5-inch bread pan and bake at 400°F for 20 minutes. Let cool slightly, then cut into slices.

If desired, you can add 1/4 cup chopped pecans or 1/4 cup cooked corn kernels to the batter.

Triple Wheat Biscuits

Sift together 1 1/4 cups all-purpose flour, 1/4 cup whole wheat pastry flour, 1/4 teaspoon salt, and 1/4 teaspoon baking soda into a mixing bowl. Stir in 1/2 cup wheat germ. Add 2 tablespoons light margarine and 2 tablespoons farmer cheese or well-drained nonfat cottage cheese and cut in until crumbly. With a fork mix in 3/4 cup buttermilk. Turn out and knead about 6 times. Roll 1/2-inch thick. Cut with a 2-inch cutter and bake on an ungreased baking sheet at 450°F for 8 to 10 minutes. Makes 1 dozen.

Simple Garlic Bread

Mix together 2 tablespoons olive oil, 1 large clove garlic (crushed in a garlic press), 1 teaspoon Italian Herb Blend (page 16), and a pinch salt. You can also add some minced fresh herbs, if you wish. Cut about 1/2 loaf whole-grain French bread or Italian bread into thick slices almost to the bottom.

With a pastry brush, lightly brush both sides of the slices and spread the garlic and herbs around on the bread. Wrap the bread in aluminum foil and bake at 350°F for about 15 minutes. Serve warm.

GRAIN COOKING CHART

Grain (1 cup)	Liquid (cups)	Cooking Time (minutes)	Yield (cups)
Rice, long-grain			
White	2	15 to 20	3
Brown	2 1/2	45 to 50	3
Brown aromatics	2–2 1/2	40 to 45	3 1/2
Rice, short-grain			
White	2	15	2
Brown	3	50	2 1/4
Barley			
Pearl	3	35 to 40	3 to 4
Pearl	(presoaked in 2 cups water)	15	3 to 4
Hulled	(presoaked in 4 1/2 cups water)	60	3
Bulgur*	2 1/2	20	3
Millet*	2 1/2	20	3
Wheat berries	(presoaked in 3 1/2 cups water)	60	2
Wild rice	3	50 to 60	3 to 4

*Allow the grains to stand, covered, for 10 minutes after they have finished cooking. Millet is greatly improved in taste if you brown it first (dry, no fat in the pan) for about 5 minutes before cooking.

LEGUME COOKING CHART

Legumes	Regular Cooking	Pressure Cooking
Black beans, kidney beans, pinto beans	2 hours	20–25 minutes
Soybeans	2 1/2 hours	30 minutes
Red beans (adzuki)	3 hours	30–35 minutes
Chickpeas (garbanzos)	3 hours	30–35 minutes
Black-eyed peas, split peas, lentils	1 hour	10–15 minutes
Red lentils	10 minutes	

SKILLET DISHES

The basic stir-fry is quick, uses fresh foods, and probably offers the most adaptability in cooking methods and use of ingredients. If you have a wok, this is the time to use it. Just heat the oil until it is quite hot and then stir-fry the various ingredients, pushing them up the side of the wok as they finish cooking. The stir-fry is then served over hot rice—short-grain and slightly sticky in the true Asian tradition—or Asian noodles.

Also included in the skillet dishes are popular grain dishes, including pilaf and risotto. Much has been written about true risotto (see page 58). A simpler stove-top meal, however, is grain pilaf, in which the grains are browned in oil with vegetables; then the liquid is added all at once and the dish cooks, undisturbed, until the grains are done, usually within half an hour.

Remember that the skillet dishes represent probably the quickest-cooking meals you will find in this book. They are particularly valuable because of the large amounts of complex carbohydrates found in the whole grains and pastas used.

Note on cooking pasta: Because much of the pasta recommended in these recipes does not come in a package necessarily, here are general indications for cooking it. Use a large pot. Heat the water (4 quarts per 1 pound pasta) to a rolling boil. Add 1/4 teaspoon salt for each 2 quarts water and a small amount of olive oil or canola oil. Add the pasta to the boiling water and stir vigorously with a wooden spoon to separate it. Reduce the heat to medium-low and cook, boiling, until the pasta reaches what the Italians call al dente, that is, cooked but firm and slightly resistant to the bite. This takes between 5 and 10 minutes depending on the type of pasta used. Lift out a piece or strand to test it. Pour immediately into a colander and shake well to get rid of the water. If using with a sauce, serve at once.

BEEF WITH BROCCOLI AND RED PEPPERS

This Asian-style dish is easily and quickly made. Serve it over hot short-grain brown or white rice. Begin the meal with a quick Chinese vegetable soup, made by heating 4 cups water, 1 can sliced mushrooms, 1 can sliced water chestnuts, 1/4 cup sliced bamboo shoots, 2 sliced green onions, 1 tablespoon low-sodium soy sauce, and 1 tablespoon dry sherry. Chilled beer is a good accompaniment.

1 tablespoon vegetable oil
12 ounces top round steak, cut into thin
   strips
4 cups small broccoli pieces (stems and
   florets)
1 large red bell pepper, cut into strips
1 large clove garlic, sliced thin
¼ cup low-sodium soy sauce

1 tablespoon cornstarch
¼ teaspoon freshly ground white pepper
½ cup Beef Stock (page 11)
1 cup water
3 to 4 cups hot cooked rice

In a large skillet over medium heat, warm the oil. Add the meat and brown slightly. Stir in the broccoli, bell pepper, garlic, and soy sauce. Cover the pan and let simmer until the vegetables are barely tender (about 8 minutes).

Blend the cornstarch and ground pepper into the stock. Add to the meat mixture along with the water and green onion. Cook, stirring constantly, until the sauce is thickened. Serve immediately over the hot rice.

Serves 6 to 8.

SUKIYAKI

Serve this easy and delicious Japanese dish with a salad of bean sprouts and cucumber and zesty Sesame Dressing (page 15).

12 ounces beef flank steak, cut 1 inch
    thick, frozen for 30 minutes
4 tablespoons dry white wine, divided
4 tablespoons low-sodium soy sauce,
    divided
1 ½ cups Beef Stock (page 11)
1 tablespoon sugar
1 tablespoon vegetable oil
2 medium carrots, cut into ½-inch
    diagonal slices
2 stalks celery, cut into ½-inch diagonal
    slices
¼ pound fresh mushrooms, sliced
4 green onions, cut into 1-inch pieces
8 ounces fine rice noodles (rice sticks)

4 cups packed spinach leaves, rinsed,
    stemmed, and torn into bite-size pieces

Cut the briefly frozen beef into ⅛-inch-thick slices and place in a bowl. Add 2 tablespoons of the wine and 2 tablespoons of the soy sauce; stir well. Let marinate while preparing the vegetables.

Combine the stock and sugar with the remaining 2 tablespoons wine and 2 tablespoons soy sauce. In a large skillet over medium heat, warm the oil. Sauté the onions, carrots, celery, mushrooms, and green onions. Add the stock mixture and noodles and simmer for 8 minutes. Stir in the meat and marinade and cook until the meat loses its red color. Add the spinach and cook for 2 minutes longer. Serve hot.

Serves 4.

CURRIED BEEF AND RICE

1 cup uncooked long-grain brown rice
12 ounces lean top round steak or lamb,
  all visible fat removed, or tempeh
1 tablespoon curry powder
¼ teaspoon salt
Generous dash cayenne pepper
1 teaspoon canola oil
1 cup coarsely chopped onion
2 cloves garlic, minced
1 cup Beef Stock (page 11)
2 cups low-sodium canned tomatoes,
  with juice
½ cup raisins
¼ cup chopped unsalted roasted peanuts

Measure the rice into a large bowl and add enough boiling water to cover. Set aside.

Cut the meat or tempeh (about 1 ½ cups) into small cubes. Combine the curry, salt, and cayenne and mix well; reserve 1 teaspoon and sprinkle the remaining mixture evenly over the steak.

In a large skillet with a lid, warm the oil over medium-high heat. Add the steak and cook until it loses its pink color (about 4 minutes). Remove the steak from the skillet and set aside.

Add the onion and garlic to the skillet and sauté for several minutes. Drain the rice and add it to the skillet along with the reserved 1 teaspoon curry mixture, stock, and tomatoes. Cover and bring to a boil, then reduce the heat and simmer until the liquid is absorbed (about 30 minutes).

Add the raisins and reserved steak and stir well. Turn off the heat and let stand, covered, for 5 minutes. Top with the peanuts and serve.

Serves 6.

Macaroni alla Napoletana

This Italian dish has been a family favorite for years. It is very quick and nourishing. If possible, use fresh beans (broad flat Italian beans are the best) and flat-leaf (Italian) parsley. The dish is delicious with garlic bread and light Italian red wine.

½ pound lean ground beef
2 ounces mild Italian turkey sausage or Italian sweet sausage, skin removed, cut into small pieces
8 ounces elbow macaroni, small shells, or spirals
½ cup chopped onion
1 large clove garlic, minced
1 ½ cups low-sodium canned tomatoes, with juice
1 cup cut green beans, fresh or frozen
1 tablespoon chopped parsley
1 teaspoon Italian Herb Blend (page 16)
½ teaspoon salt (less if the tomatoes contain salt)
½ teaspoon freshly ground black pepper, or more as needed
1 ½ cups Vegetable Stock (page 12) or water
4 ounces part-skim mozzarella cheese, diced very small

In a large skillet with a lid, brown the ground beef and sausage over medium heat, stirring to break up the meat. Remove the meat from the pan, spread on paper towels, and blot most of the fat with paper towels. Add the macaroni, onion, and garlic to the pan and brown them until golden. Then return the meat to the pan and add the tomatoes, beans, parsley, herb blend, salt, ground pepper, and stock. Cover and simmer for 25 minutes.

Taste and add more ground pepper if desired. Stir in the mozzarella and serve immediately.

Serves 4.

PILAF, GREEK STYLE

Unlike the usual pilaf, the rice in this one is already cooked, and meat is added. Serve this with a classic Greek salad of greens, black olives, and feta cheese with a simple lemon and olive oil dressing. Accompany it with hearty red wine.

¾ pound lean ground beef or lamb, or 1
    cup roasted lamb, in chunks
1 cup chopped onion
1 large clove garlic, minced
1 cup sliced celery
1 ½ cups thinly sliced zucchini
2 cups chopped tomato
2 teaspoons dried oregano
1 teaspoon dried dill weed
½ teaspoon salt
½ teaspoon freshly ground black pepper
1 package (10 ounces) frozen chopped
    spinach
3 cups cooked brown rice
½ cup quick-cooking rolled oats

Vegetable Stock (page 12) or tomato juice,
    as needed
2 tablespoons grated Romano cheese
Lemon wedges, for garnish

In a large skilled or flameproof casserole with a lid, brown the meat with the onion and garlic over medium heat. Stir in the celery, zucchini, tomato, oregano, dill, salt, ground pepper, and frozen spinach. Cover and simmer until the spinach is defrosted and the vegetables are tender.

Add the cooked rice and rolled oats; cover and cook for about 5 minutes. If the dish seems too dry, add vegetable stock or tomato juice.

Serve with the cheese sprinkled over the top and with the lemon wedges, which should be squeezed over the dish to add a lemon-juice garnish.

Serves 6 generously.

SWEDISH MEATBALLS AND PILAF

Meatballs have always been a popular and tasty way to extend the meat in a recipe. They often are added to a tomato sauce for pasta. This meatball dish with vegetables and a slightly creamy sauce has many ingredients but is quickly and easily made. Good accompaniments would be hearty rye bread and cole slaw with diced apple, orange sections, and seedless grapes and topped with Sesame Dressing (page 15). If you prefer a simpler meal, omit the Caper Sauce.

¾ pound lean ground beef
½ cup wheat germ
¼ cup dry whole wheat bread crumbs
¾ cup skim milk
¼ cup finely chopped onion
¼ cup egg substitute or 1 egg, beaten
1 tablespoon Worcestershire sauce
¼ teaspoon salt
¼ teaspoon freshly ground black pepper
1 large onion, sliced thin and separated
   into rings
1 cup Beef Stock (page 11), or more as
   needed
½ pound sliced fresh mushrooms

2 cups frozen or fresh peas
1 ½ cups cooked brown rice

Caper Sauce
1 tablespoon all-purpose flour
½ cup skim milk
½ cup plain low-fat or nonfat yogurt
2 tablespoons drained capers
¼ teaspoon salt

In a large bowl prepare the meatballs: Combine the ground beef, wheat germ, bread crumbs, skim milk, chopped onion, egg substitute, Worcestershire sauce, salt, and ground pepper; mix well.

Shape the mixture into 18 balls. Place them in the center of a large skillet or flame-proof casserole with a lid. Distribute the onion rings around them and cook over medium heat until the meatballs are brown and the onions are golden. Reduce the heat and add the stock. Deglaze the pan by scraping up the browned bits from the bottom and stirring. Add the mushrooms and peas, cover, and simmer for about 15 minutes.

While the meatballs are cooking, prepare the sauce: In a small saucepan over medium heat, combine the flour and milk and cook, stirring constantly, until thickened. Reduce the heat and stir in the yogurt, capers, and salt. Keep warm but do not boil.

Add the rice to the meatballs and vegetables and cook just long enough to heat the rice thoroughly. Pour the sauce over the top and stir well. Add more stock if the mixture is too dry. Serve hot.

Serves 6

Variations

Turkey Meatballs and Pilaf. Instead of the ground beef, use ½ pound lean ground turkey and ¼ cup textured vegetable protein or vegetable burger mix (available at your health food store; omit the salt), softened in stock or water. Use Vegetable Stock (page 12) instead of Beef Stock.

Meatballs with Bulgur. Substitute 1 ½ cups cooked bulgur for the brown rice.

Texas Meatball Stew with Rice. Substitute 1 ½ teaspoons chili powder for the Worcestershire sauce. Instead of mushrooms and peas, use 1 can (16 ounces) tomatoes with juice, 2 cups fresh or frozen corn kernels, and 1 large green bell pepper. Omit the Caper Sauce and serve right from the stew pot with Skinny Corn Bread (page 17).

Veal Shanks à la Grecque

Veal is an expensive meat, but the shanks are reasonably priced and rich in protein. Cut away any visible fat and enjoy these unusual flavors. Serve this with Simple Garlic Bread (page 18) and a spinach and mixed green salad with lemon and olive oil dressing.

All-purpose flour, for dredging
¼ teaspoon salt
¼ teaspoon freshly ground white pepper
2 tablespoons olive oil
3 ½ pounds veal shank, bone in, cut crosswise into 2-inch pieces
1 cup finely chopped onion
1 cup finely chopped celery
1 large clove garlic, minced
2 ¼ cups Chicken Stock (page 11)
1 cup chopped tomato, fresh or canned
1 cup thinly sliced zucchini
1 cup thinly sliced summer squash
½ cup dry white wine
2 tablespoons finely chopped fresh dill weed or 2 teaspoons dried dill weed
1 bay leaf
¼ cup orzo or short-grain white rice

Season the flour with the salt and ground pepper, and dredge the veal in it. In a large heavy skillet with a lid, warm the oil over medium heat. Brown the veal, turning often. Pour the fat from the skillet, then scatter the onion, celery, and garlic around the meat. Cook, stirring, until the vegetables are soft.

Add ½ cup of the stock and stir to scrape up the browned bits on the bottom and sides of the skillet. Add the tomato, zucchini, squash, wine, dill, and bay leaf. Cover closely and simmer for 30 minutes. Then add the remaining 1 ¾ cups stock and the orzo stirring well. Cover closely and cook for 15 minutes longer. Discard the bay leaf before serving.

Serves 6.

PORK CHOPS BRAISED IN BEER
WITH RED CABBAGE

Here is a leaner and quicker-cooking version of a traditional German dinner. It makes a hearty winter meal served with thick slices of dark rye bread and chilled beer.

4 center-cut pork chops, bone in, each
   1 ¼ inches thick (about 2 pounds total),
   all visible fat removed
½ teaspoon salt, or more as needed
½ teaspoon freshly ground black pepper,
   or more as needed
1 tablespoon canola oil
1 large red onion, sliced thin
1 tablespoon Dijon mustard
1 small head red cabbage, cored and sliced
   thin
1 large Granny Smith apple, cored and
   sliced thin lengthwise
2 large potatoes, sliced thin
1 cup beer
1 ½ teaspoons caraway seeds
½ teaspoon dried summer savory
¼ cup Chicken Stock (page 18)

Sprinkle the pork chops with the salt and ground pepper. In a large skillet with a lid, warm the oil over medium heat. Brown the chops on both sides (about 8 minutes in all). Remove the chops, cover, and keep warm.

Add the onion to the skillet and sauté until soft (about 2 minutes). Add the mustard, cabbage, and apple, sauté until the cabbage is lightly browned (about 2 minutes).

Add potatoes, beer, and caraway seeds, bring to a boil, and simmer until the cabbage wilts (about 4 minutes).

Return the pork chops to the skillet, covering them with the cabbage mixture. Add the savory and stock. Cover and simmer until the chops are done (about 20 minutes). Season with more salt and ground pepper, if desired. Serve immediately.

Serves 4 generously.

THAI PORK WITH CELLOPHANE NOODLES

Cellophane noodles (also called Chinese vermicelli) are made from mung beans and are transparent before they are cooked. You can find them, and the fermented black beans called for here, in Asian markets.

¾ cup cellophane noodles

5 tablespoons Vegetable Stock (page 12)

2 tablespoons fermented black beans, rinsed and chopped

1 tablespoon sweet rice vinegar

2 teaspoons cornstarch

1 large clove garlic, minced

1 thin slice fresh ginger, peeled and minced

½ pound lean pork tenderloin, all visible fat removed, sliced very thin

1 cup shredded fresh spinach

½ cup slivered red bell pepper

½ cup chopped water chestnuts

In a large mixing bowl cover the noodles with boiling water and let soak for 20 minutes. Drain and cut into 1-inch pieces with scissors. Set aside.

In a small bowl combine 2 tablespoons of the stock with the beans, vinegar, and cornstarch. Set aside.

In a wok or sauté pan over medium heat, warm the remaining 3 tablespoons stock. Add the garlic and ginger and cook for 2 minutes. Stir in the pork and reserved noodles and simmer until the pork is cooked through (about 3 minutes). Add the spinach, bell pepper, water chestnuts, and reserved bean mixture. Cook until the sauce is clear, tossing to heat all the ingredients. Serve immediately.

Serves 4.

RAGOÛT OF HAM AND BEANS

Prepare the soybeans ahead of time and this easy dish is quickly made. Serve with tossed green salad topped with Creamy Orange Dressing (page 15) and crusty French bread.

1 cup ham chunks (turkey ham is excellent)
2 medium onions, cut into wedges
2 tablespoons canola oil
4 carrots, cut into ¼-inch rounds
2 stalks celery, with tops, chopped
3 cloves garlic, peeled and minced
3 tablespoons Tomato Purée (page 14) or
    tomato paste
1 tablespoon low-sodium soy sauce
1 cup Vegetable Stock (page 12) *or* liquid
    from beans

3 cups cooked soybeans
1 large potato, diced
1 tomato, chopped
1 teaspoon crushed sage
½ teaspoon dried marjoram

In a large Dutch oven sauté the ham chunks and onions in the oil over medium heat until the onion softens, about 5 minutes. Reduce the heat and add the carrots, celery, and garlic. Stir and cook for 2 minutes.

Blend the tomato purée, soy sauce, and stock. Add to the pot along with the remaining ingredients. Cover and simmer until the vegetables are tender, about 30 minutes.

Serves 6.

POLENTA WITH PEPPERS AND SAUSAGE

This meal is hearty and quick. Serve it with a green salad and Light Herb Dressing (page 15).

1 tablespoon olive oil
3 green onions, chopped
½ green bell pepper, cut into short strips
½ red bell pepper, cut into short strips
¼ pound Italian sweet sausage or turkey sausage, cut into ½-inch pieces
2 ¼ cups skim milk
¾ cup cornmeal
1 teaspoon dried basil
2 tablespoons Parmesan or Romano cheese
Salt and pepper to taste

In a medium skillet warm the oil over medium heat. Add the onion and peppers and cook about 5 minutes. Stir in the sausage pieces and cook, stirring, until the sausage is thoroughly cooked, about 5 minutes.

In a large pot with a cover, slowly heat the milk to boiling. Whisk in the cornmeal gradually, beating all the time. Continue to beat until the mixture is smooth and thick, about 5 minutes. Cover the pot and allow it to cook about 10 minutes. Stir again. Add the sausage mixture and the remaining ingredients. Taste and season with salt and pepper.

Spoon the polenta out into wide flat bowls. Garnish with additional cheese, if desired.

Serves 4 to 6.

Cannellini e Pepperoni

This combination of legumes, greens, and pasta represents Italian country cooking at its best. Use pepperoni made from turkey, if at all possible. Serve this with beer or red wine and crusty whole-grain country bread. Note that the dried beans must be soaked overnight before using.

2 cans (19 ounces each) cannellini,
    rinsed and drained, or 1 pound
    dried cannellini beans
3 pounds Swiss chard or collard greens
1 tablespoon olive oil
5 cloves garlic, chopped fine
¼ pound pepperoni, sliced thin and cut in
    half
¼ cup chopped flat-leaf parsley
1 tablespoon chopped fresh oregano or 1
    teaspoon dried oregano
1 cup uncooked vegetable spiral pasta or
    elbow macaroni
¾ cup Vegetable Stock (page 12)
1 ½ cups water
Salt and freshly ground pepper, to taste

If using dried beans, pour boiling water over them and soak overnight; drain thoroughly.

Trim the Swiss chard and blanch in boiling water for 2 minutes. Drain and chop coarsely.

In a heavy pot with a lid, warm the oil over medium heat. Sauté the garlic until golden. Add the pepperoni, parsley, and oregano and sauté for 1 minute. Add the pasta, stock, water, reserved chard, and beans (see Note). Taste and adjust the seasoning (the amount of salt needed depends a great deal on the pepperoni used).

Cover and cook over low heat for 15 to 20 minutes, stirring occasionally. Serve hot.

Serves 6 to 8.

Note: If using dried beans, increase the cooking time to 45 minutes.

LINGUINI WITH CHICKEN AND ZUCCHINI

This is one of the simplest pasta sauces ever. If you have any leftover cooked chicken, your meal can be ready in just a few minutes. Serve it with Simple Garlic Bread (page 18) and a salad of mixed greens and tomato wedges.

1 tablespoon olive oil
1 medium onion, chopped
1 large clove garlic, minced
¼ pound fresh mushrooms, sliced
½ cup water
1 cup finely chopped cooked chicken
1 teaspoon rubbed dried sage
½ teaspoon salt
½ teaspoon freshly ground white pepper
½ cup dry white wine
2 cups cubed zucchini (¼-inch pieces)
8 ounces linguini, flat spinach pasta, or
    whole wheat spirals
3 quarts water
4 tablespoons Romano cheese

In a heavy skillet with a lid, warm the oil over medium heat. Add the onion, garlic, and mushrooms and sauté until the onions are transparent. Stir in the water, chicken, sage, salt, pepper, wine, and zucchini. Cover and steam for 5 minutes.

Meanwhile, boil the pasta in the water until al dente (about 7 minutes). Drain and place on 4 warm serving plates or bowls. Spoon the chicken mixture over the pasta. Sprinkle the cheese over all. Serve at once.

Serves 4.

Variations

Linguini with Chicken and Fresh Tomatoes.
Instead of zucchini, use 10 ounces fresh spinach, washed, stems removed, torn into pieces, and 2 large tomatoes, cut into pieces. Reduce the water to ¼ cup and substitute 1 teaspoon dried basil for the sage. Steam about 4 minutes.

Linguini with Turkey and Zucchini.
Substitute cooked turkey for the chicken.

HERBED CHICKEN AND RICE, VENETIAN STYLE

The popular combination of rice and peas called risi e bisi *is eaten all over Western Europe. In northern Italy the dish is more like a soup. The adaptation here uses less liquid and adds chicken to make a complete meal (see Note). You could accompany it with a* macedonia *(a combination of mixed fresh fruits) and crisp white wine.*

1 tablespoon canola oil

3 green onions, chopped fine

1 cup short-grain white rice

½ teaspoon dried crushed basil or 1 ½ teaspoons minced fresh basil

½ teaspoon dried lemon thyme or 1 teaspoon minced fresh lemon thyme

2 ½ cups Chicken Stock (page 11), heated

2 chicken breast quarters (about 12 ounces each), skin and all visible fat removed

2 cups frozen tiny peas

¼ cup grated Parmesan cheese

In a heavy skillet or pot with a lid, warm the canola oil over medium heat. Sauté the green onions and rice, stirring, until the rice is golden. Gently stir in the basil, thyme, and stock. Reduce the heat, cover, and simmer for 15 minutes.

With a sharp knife cut the chicken meat from the bone and into strips (about 2 inches long and ¼ inch wide). Add it to the pot, stir well, cover, and cook until the chicken is steamed through and tender (about 10 minutes).

Stir in the peas (it is not necessary to defrost them) and cook just enough to heat them thoroughly (no more than 2 minutes). Remove the pot from the heat, sprinkle the cheese over all, toss lightly to fluff the rice, and serve immediately.

Serves 6.

Note: This dish can also be made as a risotto, by adding the stock in three parts and stirring frequently. For this method, see page 58.

Variations

Herbed Pork with Rice. Use pork instead of chicken: Sauté 1 cup pork in strips (either fresh from the loin or leftover from a roast, all visible fat removed) in the canola oil before adding the green onions and rice. Substitute 1 teaspoon summer savory for the basil. Proceed as above.

Wehani Rice with Chicken. Omit the herbs and Parmesan cheese. Sauté 1 small carrot, sliced, with the onions and substitute 2 cups Wehani rice for the white rice. When adding the chicken, stir in ¼ cup port wine, ¼ teaspoon each salt and freshly ground white pepper, and 2 tablespoons minced parsley. Garnish with ⅓ cup chopped pecans, toasted.

CHICKEN WITH CASHEWS

This Chinese dish, called U Quo Chow Gai Ding, *provides the opportunity to do an authentic stir-fry. Although there are several separate receptacles involved, everything eventually is combined and cooked in one pan. The secret is to assemble all the ingredients before you start to cook. Serve this dish with lots of hot short-grain rice, preferably brown, and hot tea.*

2 tablespoons cornstarch
1 tablespoon dry sherry
1 teaspoon low-sodium soy sauce
1 inch piece fresh ginger, peeled and
   minced
1 medium chicken breast quarter (about 8
   ounces), skinned, boned, and cut into
   ½-inch cubes
¼ pound fresh mushrooms, sliced
Half a 5-ounce can water chestnuts,
   drained and sliced
Half an 8-ounce can sliced bamboo
   shoots, drained and cut into ½-inch
   cubes
1 cup (about 3 ounces) snow peas cut in
   half, ends trimmed
¾ cup Chicken Stock (page 11)
1 tablespoon peanut oil
¼ cup whole raw cashews
¼ teaspoon salt
1 large clove garlic, minced
1 large onion, halved, then sliced
4 cups hot cooked short-grain brown rice

In a medium bowl combine 1 tablespoon of the cornstarch, the sherry, soy sauce, and fresh ginger. Stir in the chicken and set aside to marinate for at least 15 minutes.

In a large bowl combine the mushrooms, water chestnuts, bamboo shoots, and snow peas; set aside. In a 1-cup measure mix together the stock and the remaining 1 tablespoon cornstarch; set aside.

In a wok or sauté pan over medium heat, warm the oil until hot. Add the nuts and stir-fry until lightly browned. (Watch carefully; this happens quickly.) Remove the nuts with a slotted spoon and set aside. Add the salt, garlic, and onion and stir-fry until they are golden.

Add the reserved chicken mixture and stir until the chicken starts to brown (about 3 minutes). Add the reserved vegetables and stir for 2 minutes. Add the reserved stock mixture and stir until it comes to a boil and thickens. Turn off the heat, cover the pan, and let the mixture stand for 2 to 3 minutes. Stir in the reserved cashews and serve immediately on the hot rice.

Serves 4.

TURKEY STROGANOFF

Traditionally this dish is made with thin strips of beef and sour cream. This updated version uses leaner ingredients: turkey and low-fat yogurt. Accompany it with a salad of thinly sliced cucumbers, chilled in a yogurt sauce (1 clove garlic, crushed and mixed with 2 cups plain low-fat yogurt and 1/4 teaspoon chopped dried mint), and dark Russian rye bread.

1 tablespoon canola oil
1 medium onion, chopped
½ pound fresh mushrooms, sliced
1 tablespoon all-purpose flour
2 teaspoons paprika
½ teaspoon salt
½ teaspoon dried basil
¼ teaspoon dried thyme
½ cup Chicken or Turkey Stock
   (pages 11–12)
½ cup dry white wine
½ cup plain low-fat or nonfat yogurt
2 cups diced cooked turkey breast or veal
2 teaspoons lemon juice
2 tablespoons chopped fresh dill weed or
   2 teaspoons dried dill weed

6 ounces light egg noodles, cooked,
   drained, and kept hot

In a large saucepan or Dutch oven over medium heat, warm the oil. Add the onion and sauté until golden. Add the mushrooms and cook, stirring, for 3 to 5 minutes.

Blend in the flour, paprika, salt, basil, and thyme. Gradually stir in the stock and wine. Cook, stirring constantly, until the mixture thickens and bubbles for a minute; then cover and simmer for 5 minutes. Remove from the heat.

Blend in the yogurt. Add the turkey, lemon juice, and dill. Heat thoroughly over low heat but do not boil. Serve over the hot noodles.

Serves 4.

Note: If you use veal, cut it into thin strips and sauté with the onion.

TURKEY CURRY

This dish is my favorite way of using turkey left over from the holidays. It is invariably delicious, and very quickly made. You can serve the usual curry accompaniments—grated coconut (but use only sparingly, please, since it is high in saturated fat) and chopped unsalted roasted peanuts. Start cooking the rice accompaniment about 40 minutes before you start making the curry so that everything will be done at the same time.

1 tablespoon canola oil
1 large onion, chopped fine
1 cup thinly sliced celery
1 tart apple, cored and chopped
½ teaspoon minced peeled fresh ginger or
    ½ teaspoon ground ginger
2 tablespoons all-purpose flour
1 tablespoon curry powder
⅛ teaspoon ground cumin

2 cups Turkey Stock (page 12)
3 cups shredded cooked turkey
½ cup raisins
3 cups hot cooked long-grain brown rice

In a large stovetop casserole with a lid, warm the oil over medium heat. Sauté the onion, celery, apple, and fresh ginger until tender, but not browned. (If you use ground ginger, add it with the curry.) Sprinkle the flour, curry, and cumin over the top and cook, stirring, for 2 minutes.

Stir in the stock and bring to a boil, stirring constantly. Cook until thickened. Add the turkey and heat thoroughly; do not boil. Stir in the raisins. Serve immediately over the hot rice.

Serves 6.

Turkey Ham and Pineapple, Hawaiian Style

This dish is low in fat and high in flavor. Be sure to use unsweetened pineapple, and turkey ham. Serve it with a mixed green salad topped with Light Herb Dressing (page 15).

1 tablespoon canola oil

1 cup diagonally sliced carrot (¼ inch thick)

1 cup diagonally sliced celery

3 green onions, diagonally sliced into 1-inch pieces

1 large clove garlic, minced

1 teaspoon minced peeled fresh ginger

1 can (8 ounces) pineapple chunks, drained and juice reserved

1 teaspoon cornstarch

1 tablespoon low-sodium soy sauce

1 teaspoon lemon juice

1 teaspoon Chinese five-spice powder

½ teaspoon freshly ground white pepper

2 cups diced turkey ham (½-inch pieces)

1 can (5 ounces) water chestnuts, drained and sliced thin

4 cups hot cooked short-grain brown rice

In a flameproof casserole with a lid, warm the oil over medium heat. Add the carrot, celery, green onions, garlic, and fresh ginger. Sauté until the vegetables are crisp-tender. Remove from the heat and set aside.

Measure the pineapple juice into a 2-cup measure. Add enough water to make 1 ¼ cups. Blend in the cornstarch, soy sauce, lemon juice, spice powder, and ground pepper. Stir into the reserved vegetable mixture and cook, stirring, until thickened.

Add the pineapple, ham, and water chestnuts. Heat thoroughly. Serve over the hot rice.

Serves 6.

COD, SPANISH STYLE

This dish is traditionally made with hake, Spain's most popular fish. This adaptation uses cod, which is a member of the same family. For a complete meal, serve it with a mixed green salad and dry white wine.

1 ½ pounds new potatoes, sliced thin
1 tablespoon olive oil
2 large cloves garlic, minced
1 large onion, sliced
4 medium carrots, sliced fine
4 tablespoons Crushed Tomatoes
    (page 14) or tomato paste
1 tablespoon white wine vinegar
1 cup dry white wine
1 cup water
1 bay leaf
1 teaspoon dried thyme
½ teaspoon salt
½ teaspoon cayenne pepper
4 cod steaks (each 4 to 6 ounces), about
    1 inch thick, rinsed and patted dry
3 tablespoons chopped parsley

In a medium saucepan over medium-high heat, steam the potatoes in a small amount of water until tender (about 10 minutes).

Meanwhile, in a nonstick skillet with a lid, warm the oil over medium-high heat. Sauté the garlic, onion, and carrots until the onion softens. Stir in the tomatoes, vinegar, wine, water, bay leaf, thyme, salt, and cayenne. Cover, reduce the heat, and let simmer. Drain the cooked potatoes and add them to the onion mixture.

Place the fish in the skillet, under the vegetables and sauce, and cook for about 10 minutes. Discard the bay leaf, sprinkle the parsley on top, and serve.

Serves 4.

Variation

Haddock, Spanish Style. Substitute 4 haddock fillets or red snapper fillets (4 to 6 ounces each) for the cod.

TUNA SPAGHETTI WITH YOGURT

This quick and easy pasta dish is a rather unusual combination of tuna and yogurt. Serve it with a salad of mixed greens, including shredded spinach, and dry white wine or chilled beer.

1 cup plain nonfat yogurt
2 large cloves garlic, minced
½ teaspoon salt, divided
2 tablespoons olive oil
4 medium onions, chopped fine
6 medium tomatoes, chopped
1 tablespoon chopped fresh basil or
    1 teaspoon dried basil
¼ teaspoon freshly ground black pepper
1 pound whole wheat or imported semolina
    spaghetti
2 cans (6 ½ ounces each) water-packed
    chunk light tuna, drained and flaked
Parsley, for garnish

In a small bowl blend the yogurt, garlic, and ¼ teaspoon of the salt; set aside.

In a medium saucepan over medium heat, warm the oil. Sauté the onions until they are soft but not browned. Add the tomatoes, the remaining ¼ teaspoon salt, basil, and ground pepper; simmer for 20 minutes.

While the sauce is cooking, cook the spaghetti until al dente (see page 21). Drain and pour into a large bowl or spaghetti plate.

Stir the tuna into the tomato sauce, then mix the sauce into the pasta, stirring until the pasta is coated with sauce. Pour the reserved yogurt mixture over the top or drizzle a little over each portion. Garnish with parsley and serve.

Serves 6.

Tuna and Couscous Niçoise

The garlic and olives give this dish its name. If you cannot find Niçoise olives (French olives, tiny and dark brown), use Greek black olives. Serve with chunks of French bread and chilled beer.

1 ¼ cups Chicken Stock (page 11)
¼ teaspoon salt
2 large cloves garlic, minced
1 teaspoon olive oil
1 ½ cups medium-grain couscous
2 cups cut-up fresh green beans (1-inch pieces)
1 can (6 ½ ounces) chunk tuna in water, drained and flaked
2 large tomatoes, peeled and chopped fine
¼ cup Niçoise olives, pitted and sliced
8 large leaves fresh basil, julienned
1 tablespoon coarsely chopped parsley

1 tablespoon white wine vinegar, preferably tarragon
¼ teaspoon freshly ground black pepper

In a stovetop casserole with a tight-fitting lid, combine the stock, salt, garlic, and oil and bring to a boil over high heat. Stir in the couscous and remove from the heat. Cover and let stand for 5 minutes.

Meanwhile, cook the beans until they are crisp-tender. Uncover the casserole and fluff the couscous with a fork until the grains are separate. Stir in the beans, tuna, tomatoes, olives, basil, parsley, vinegar, and ground pepper. Heat until warmed through. Serve at once.

Serves 6.

Shrimp Sauté with Indian Spices

This quickly prepared meal combines several interesting sweet and hot spices and their fragrances. Basmati rice, also fragrant, makes the perfect accompaniment.

½ teaspoon cumin seeds
¼ teaspoon coriander seeds
1 tablespoon canola oil
1 ½ pounds large shrimp, peeled and
    deveined
⅛ teaspoon red pepper flakes
¼ teaspoon salt
¼ teaspoon freshly ground white pepper
1 shallot or 2 green onions, minced
5 cloves garlic, minced
1-inch piece fresh ginger, peeled, minced
2 teaspoons curry powder
1 can (28 ounces) whole tomatoes,
    chopped, with juice
1 red bell pepper, sliced thin
1 green bell pepper, sliced thin
1 small zucchini, cut into sticks ½ inch by
    2 ½ inches
½ cup chopped cilantro or parsley
1 tablespoon lemon juice
4 cups hot cooked brown basmati rice

In a small skillet, toast the cumin and coriander seeds until fragrant (30 to 40 seconds), shaking the pan. Let cool, then crush with a mortar and pestle. Set aside.

In a large sauté pan or heavy skillet, heat the oil. Add the shrimp and red pepper flakes; sauté until the shrimp turn bright pink (2 to 3 minutes). Transfer the shrimp to a plate and season with the salt and ground pepper. Set aside.

Add the shallot, garlic, fresh ginger, curry, and reserved crushed seeds to the skillet.

Cook, stirring, until the shallot is lightly browned (about 1 minute). Stir in the tomatoes, bell peppers, and zucchini. Cook, stirring often, until the sauce thickens somewhat (8 to 10 minutes). Add the reserved shrimp, the cilantro, and lemon juice and heat through. Serve over the hot rice.

Serves 6.

Scallops Stir-fried with Fresh Ginger and Vegetables

Here is a fresh-tasting, pretty Asian dish, very quickly made. Serve it over mounds of hot short-grain rice, preferably brown.

3 teaspoons canola oil, divided
1-inch piece fresh ginger, peeled and
  minced
1 large clove garlic, minced
1 ½ cups (about 4 ounces) snow peas cut
  in half, ends trimmed
1 cup thinly sliced carrot
1 tablespoon low-sodium soy sauce
2 teaspoons cornstarch
1 pound fresh sea scallops
½ cup diagonally sliced green onion
4 cups hot cooked short-grain brown rice

In a sauté pan over medium-high heat, warm 2 teaspoons of the oil. Add the fresh ginger and garlic and stir-fry for 30 seconds. Add the snow peas and carrot and stir-fry for 1 minute. Remove the vegetables from the skillet with a slotted spoon. Set aside and keep warm.

In a small bowl combine the soy sauce and cornstarch; set aside.

Add the remaining 1 teaspoon oil to the pan along with the scallops, and stir-fry over medium heat for 3 minutes. Add the reserved vegetables, reserved soy sauce mixture, and green onion. Continue to stir and cook for 1 minute longer. Serve over the hot rice.

Serves 4.

SEAFOOD LINGUINI WITH VEGETABLES

The combination of seafood and pasta has long been a favorite in Mediterranean countries. Here is a change from tomato sauce-based combinations. Serve it with a salad of fresh sliced tomatoes on a bed of mixed greens, lots of crusty garlic bread, and dry white wine.

1 pound linguini or spaghettini
4 quarts water
1 tablespoon olive oil
3 cloves garlic, crushed in a garlic press
½ cup chopped celery, including tops
½ cup chopped onion
2 tablespoons chopped parsley
3 dozen uncooked clams in the shell, well washed
½ pound uncooked shrimp, shelled and deveined
½ pound bay scallops
½ pound fresh mushrooms, sliced
1 ½ cups tiny peas, fresh, or frozen and defrosted
½ cup dry white wine
¼ cup shredded Parmesan or Asiago cheese

In a large pot over high heat, cook the pasta in the water until al dente. Drain, rinse in hot water, and keep warm.

Meanwhile, in a large saucepan over medium heat, warm the oil. Sauté the garlic, celery, onion, and parsley. Add the clams; when they start to open, add the shrimp, scallops, mushrooms, and peas. Simmer until the shrimp are pink and the clams are fully open. Be careful not to overcook. Stir in the white wine and heat through.

Transfer the pasta to a large serving bowl and top with the seafood mixture. Sprinkle with the cheese, mix well, and serve on warmed plates.

Serves 6 generously.

MUSSELS WITH RICE PILAF

This dish combines several cooking traditions, in keeping with the international exchange of ideas that enhances today's cooking. Serve this simple dish with crusty French bread and a good white wine.

1 tablespoon olive oil
1 cup chopped onion
3 cloves garlic, minced
1 cup long-grain white or basmati rice
1 teaspoon dried oregano
½ teaspoon salt
¼ teaspoon freshly ground white pepper
2 cups Chicken Stock (page 11) or Fish Stock (page 12)
24 mussels, scrubbed and debearded
1 large carrot, julienned
1 cup snow peas cut in half, ends trimmed

In a large sauté pan over medium heat, warm the oil. Sauté the onion and garlic for about 5 minutes. Add the rice, oregano, salt, and ground pepper and sauté for 3 minutes more. Pour in the stock and bring to a boil. Reduce the heat, cover, and simmer for 20 minutes.

Add the mussels and carrot. Loosely cover the pan and continue cooking. When the mussels begin to open, add the snow peas. Cover and simmer until the mussels are completely open (about 6 minutes). Be careful not to overcook. Discard any mussels that don't open. Serve immediately.

Serves 4.

Vegetable Medley with Mozzarella Topping

This is an American adaptation of the German Allerei. Here is a place to use fresh herbs, if you have them in your garden. Serve thick slices of rye or whole wheat bread and chilled beer or hearty red wine.

1 tablespoon olive oil
1 large onion, sliced thin
2 red bell peppers, cut in half crosswise, then into thin lengthwise strips
2 medium potatoes, halved, then sliced thin
1 cup sliced green beans
2 small to medium zucchini (about ¾ pound total), cut into thin rounds
2 medium tomatoes, cut into 1-inch cubes
1 tablespoon minced fresh summer savory or lemon thyme or 1 teaspoon dried winter savory or thyme
½ teaspoon salt
½ teaspoon freshly ground white pepper

¼ cup whole wheat bread crumbs, toasted, or unsweetened crunchy cereal flakes, such as Kellogg's Nutri-Grain®
1 cup shredded part-skim mozzarella cheese

In a large skillet with a lid, warm the oil over medium heat. Sauté the onion for 1 minute, then add the bell peppers and cook for about 1 minute longer. Add the potatoes and beans and cook, stirring, for about 5 minutes. Stir in the zucchini, tomatoes, savory, salt, and ground pepper. Cover closely and cook, stirring occasionally, for about 10 minutes.

Remove the pan from the heat. Combine the bread crumbs and cheese; sprinkle over the vegetables. Cover and let the cheese melt, or place the skillet under the broiler until the cheese is lightly browned (about 5 minutes). Serve hot.

Serves 4 to 6.

INDONESIAN STIR-FRY

This dish is spicy hot, so be forewarned. Serve it with a salad of romaine and orange slices with Creamy Orange Dressing (page 15) and chilled beer or medium-dry white wine.

1 tablespoon peanut oil
1 hot green chile, seeded and minced
2 tablespoons minced peeled fresh ginger
4 cloves garlic, minced
1 red bell pepper, cut into strips
1 cup thinly sliced green onion
2 celery stalks, cut into diagonal slices
½ cup thinly sliced fresh mushrooms
¾ cup broccoli florets
¾ cup sliced cauliflower florets
2 cups Vegetable Stock (page 12)
½ cup unsalted peanut butter
2 tablespoons low-sodium soy sauce
1 tablespoon lemon juice
1 teaspoon honey
½ teaspoon red pepper flakes
2 cups cubed firm tofu (½-inch pieces)
3 to 4 cups hot cooked short-grain rice

In a large skillet over medium heat, warm the oil. Sauté the chile, fresh ginger, and garlic for 5 minutes. Add the bell peppers, green onion, celery, mushrooms, broccoli, and cauliflower; stir to combine.

Add 1 cup of the stock, stirring to deglaze the pan. In a 2-cup measure combine the remaining 1 cup stock, peanut butter, soy sauce, lemon juice, honey, and pepper flakes; add to the pan. Cook over medium heat, stirring constantly, until the sauce thickens and begins to simmer; then reduce the heat and add the tofu. Cover and cook until the vegetables are crisp-tender (4 to 5 minutes). Serve over the hot rice.

Serves 6.

Variation

Vietnamese Stir-fry. Omit the chile, peanut butter, lemon juice, honey, and red pepper flakes. Use only 1 cup stock and season it with 1 tablespoon rice vinegar, ½ teaspoon ground cumin, and 3 tablespoons minced cilantro.

VEGETABLE-TOPPED CRISP NOODLES

Although this Chinese dish is more complicated than many given here, it is fun and different and well worth the extra effort.

10 to 12 ounces Asian rice noodles
3 tablespoons canola oil, divided
½ teaspoon salt
1 large clove garlic, minced
1 medium onion, minced
2 tablespoons minced peeled fresh ginger
2 stalks celery, cut into thin diagonal slices
2 medium carrots, cut into thin diagonal slices
1 green or red bell pepper, cut into ¼-inch strips
1 ½ cups sliced broccoli florets and stems, kept separate, with stems cut into ¼-inch slices
¼ pound fresh mushrooms, sliced
3 tablespoons water
3 tablespoons cornstarch
2 tablespoons low-sodium soy sauce
⅛ teaspoon cayenne pepper
¼ cup dry sherry

2 ½ cups Root Vegetable Stock (page 13)
1 pound firm tofu, drained and cut into ¾-inch cubes

Cook the noodles according to package directions, then drain and toss with 1 tablespoon of the oil and the salt. Set aside.

Place a 14-inch pizza pan or a 15- by 10-inch baking sheet with a rim in a 500°F oven. When the pan is very hot, pour in 1 tablespoon of the oil and tilt to coat. Spread the cooked noodles evenly in the pan and bake uncovered on the bottom rack of the oven until golden brown (25 to 30 minutes).

About 10 minutes before the noodles are done, heat the remaining 1 tablespoon oil in a wok or a large sauté pan over medium-high heat. Add the garlic, onion, fresh ginger, celery, carrots, bell pepper, and broccoli stems and stir-fry for 2 minutes. Reduce the heat to medium and add the water. Cover and cook for 3 minutes, stirring often. Add the broccoli florets and mushrooms and stir-fry for 1 minute.

Combine the water, cornstarch, soy sauce, cayenne, sherry, and stock; stir into the pan along with the tofu. Cook until the sauce boils and thickens.

To serve, loosen the crisp noodles from the pan and slide them onto a cutting board. Cut into 6 wedges or rectangles, transfer to individual plates, and top with the vegetables and sauce.

Serves 6.

Tofu-Broccoli-Bulgur Skillet

A wonderful combination of flavors and textures, the meal goes well with a mixed green salad topped with Light Herb Dressing (page 15).

2 cups bulgur
4 cups boiling water
2 tablespoons canola oil
2 pounds firm tofu, cut into 1-inch cubes
1 large onion, cut in half and sliced
½ cup chopped raw cashews
1 tablespoon sesame seeds
2 tablespoons low-sodium soy sauce
1 teaspoon dried marjoram
3 cups broccoli florets and stems in small pieces
1 cup sliced mushrooms
3 tablespoons water

Using a large saucepan, stir the bulgur into the boiling water. Reduce the heat to low, cover, and simmer 15 minutes. Turn off the heat and keep covered on stove until ready to use.

In the meanwhile, heat the oil in a large skillet with a cover. Stir-fry the tofu, onion, cashews, and sesame seeds over medium heat for 2 minutes. Sprinkle the soy sauce and marjoram over and stir-fry for another minute. Add the broccoli, mushrooms, and water, stir, and cover. Steam until broccoli is just tender, 3 to 5 minutes.

Gently stir in the cooked bulgur, heat thoroughly, and serve with additional soy sauce, if desired.

Serves 6.

PASTA PRIMAVERA

Feel free to vary the vegetables. Just be sure to maintain a range of colors. Steam harder vegetables briefly before adding them.

1 pound whole wheat spaghetti or flat spinach pasta
⅓ cup pine nuts
1 ½ cups fresh broccoli cut into small pieces
1 cup julienned or thinly sliced carrot
1 tablespoon olive *or* canola oil
1 large clove garlic, chopped fine
4 large green onions, cut into 1 ½-inch slices
2 tablespoons chopped fresh basil *or* 1 teaspoon dried oregano
½ large green bell pepper, halved and julienned
½ red bell pepper, halved and julienned
1 cup snow peas cut in half, ends trimmed
1 cup julienned zucchini
2 large fresh tomatoes, cut into 1-inch cubes

¼ cup minced parsley
½ cup plain nonfat yogurt
½ cup grated Parmesan cheese

Cook the spaghetti in 4 quarts rapidly boiling water until al dente (see page 21). Drain and set aside, keeping it warm. Toast the pine nuts in a 350°F oven until lightly browned; set aside. Steam the broccoli and carrot until crisp-tender; set aside.

In a large sauté pan over medium heat, warm the olive oil. Sauté the garlic, green onions, basil (or oregano), bell peppers, snow peas, and zucchini until the vegetables are slightly cooked but still crisp. Add the tomatoes, parsley, yogurt, and steamed broccoli and carrot; cook until heated thoroughly.

Stir in the pine nuts and Parmesan cheese. Add the reserved pasta and toss gently to mix. Serve hot, with additional cheese if desired.

Serves 6 to 8.

BULGUR AND CHICKPEAS

This popular Middle Eastern dish is easy to make. It is best to start with dried chickpeas that you have soaked and cooked ahead of time. Serve with toasted pita bread and hearty red wine.

1 tablespoon olive oil
1 ¼ cups uncooked medium bulgur
1 medium onion, chopped
1 clove garlic, minced
1 teaspoon ground cumin
2 ½ cups Root Vegetable Stock (page 13)
½ teaspoon dried oregano
½ teaspoon dried dill weed
½ teaspoon salt
½ teaspoon freshly ground black pepper
¾ cup cooked chickpeas or canned chickpeas, rinsed and drained
1 medium zucchini, quartered and sliced thin
1 cup plain nonfat yogurt

In a large saucepan or stovetop casserole with a lid, warm the oil over medium heat. Sauté the bulgur until it is slightly browned (about 5 minutes). Add the onion, garlic, and cumin and sauté, stirring, for another 5 minutes. Stir in the stock, oregano, dill, salt, and ground pepper. Bring to a boil, then reduce the heat, cover, and simmer until the stock is absorbed (about 20 minutes).

Stir in the chickpeas and zucchini; cover and cook for 5 minutes. Stir in the yogurt and heat thoroughly. Serve hot.

Serves 6.

Variation

Bulgur and Lentils. Substitute ¾ cup cooked lentils for the chickpeas; sauté one green bell pepper with the onion and garlic. Substitute ½ teaspoon ground allspice for the oregano and dill. Stir in 2 teaspoons grated lemon zest with the yogurt. Garnish with chopped parsley, if desired.

Spirals with Fresh Tomatoes, Broccoli, and Pesto

The wonderful Italian mixture called pesto has become very popular in this country. Serve this, as well as the other pasta dishes here, with Simple Garlic Bread (page 18) or crusty Italian bread, and hearty Italian red wine.

1 pound broccoli, florets separated, stems cut crosswise into ½-inch slices
1 pound spirals or shell pasta, preferably colored vegetable pasta
1 tablespoon olive oil
1 large clove garlic, minced
2 medium tomatoes, cut into 1-inch chunks
½ teaspoon freshly ground black pepper
⅔ cup Pesto (page 15), diluted with ¼ cup boiling water
¼ cup freshly grated Parmesan or Romano cheese

In a large pot over high heat, bring 2 quarts water to a boil. Cook the broccoli for 4 minutes. Remove it with a slotted spoon and keep warm.

In the same pot, add 2 more quarts water, bring it to a rolling boil, and cook the pasta until al dente (see page 21).

Meanwhile, in a large skillet over medium heat, warm the oil. Add the garlic and cook until brown. Add the cooked broccoli, tossing gently until it is heated through. Add the tomatoes and ground pepper, remove from the heat, and cover.

Drain the pasta and arrange it in a large, shallow, heated dish. Pour the reserved broccoli and tomatoes over the top. Top with the diluted Pesto and toss gently. Pass the cheese to sprinkle over individual portions.

Risotto Pomodoro con le Zucchine

True risotto is a northern Italian dish made with arborio, a short-grain Italian white rice; it is cooked with the liquid added in stages until the rice reaches a creamy yet al dente consistency. The Italians serve this as a first course before the veal, chicken, or roast. This particular version is complete by itself, or you can add chopped ham or sweet sausage, or strips of chicken breast (about 1/2 pound in all cases). Accompany it with the light mixed green salad and dry white wine.

2 tablespoons olive oil, divided
3 tablespoons coarsely chopped onion
3 large cloves garlic, minced
4 medium or 6 small zucchini, sliced into
  ½-inch-thick rounds
Pinch salt
4 ½ to 5 cups Vegetable Stock (page 12)
1 ½ cups uncooked arborio or other
  short-grain white rice
3 medium tomatoes, chopped
Freshly ground black pepper, to taste
1 tablespoon minced flat-leaf (Italian)
  parsley

3 tablespoons grated Parmesan cheese,
  plus more for serving

In a large Dutch oven or heavy stovetop casserole with a lid, warm 1 tablespoon of the oil over medium-high heat. Sauté the onion until it becomes translucent. Add the garlic; as soon as it colors slightly, stir in the zucchini. Reduce the heat to medium-low, add the salt, and cook until the zucchini reaches a rich golden color (about 20 minutes).

Meanwhile, in a large saucepan over medium-low heat, warm the stock to a slow, steady simmer.

Add the remaining 1 tablespoon oil to the zucchini in the Dutch oven and increase the heat to high. When the zucchini begins to bubble, add the rice and stir until it is well coated. Sauté lightly for about 1 minute, then reduce the heat to medium-low and add ½ cup of the simmering stock. Stir while cooking until the rice absorbs the liquid. When the rice dries out, add another ½ cup stock and continue to stir as the rice cooks. Stir in the tomatoes.

You must be tireless in your stirring of the rice mixture, always loosening the rice from the entire bottom surface of the pot. Keep adding liquid as the rice dries out, but be patient and don't drown the rice. Be sure that the cooking heat is right—hot enough to reduce the liquid but slow enough for the rice to cook evenly.

When the rice is done, taste for seasoning. Remember that the Parmesan that you will be adding is salty. Turn off the heat, grind a few turns of the pepper mill over everything, and add the minced parsley and Parmesan; mix thoroughly. Serve immediately with more freshly grated Parmesan on the side.

Serves 4.

Variations

Risotto Primavera. About 10 minutes before the rice is done, stir in 1 small carrot, cut into ¼-inch dice; 1 cup asparagus pieces (1 ½ inches long), blanched; 1 cup sugar snap peas cut in half, strings and stems removed; and 1 cup thinly sliced spinach leaves, rinsed. Serves 6.

Risotto with Salmon and Peas. Omit the zucchini. Add the rice to the pot after you have sautéed the onion and garlic. With the last addition of liquid, stir in 12 ounces salmon fillet, cut into cubes, and 2 cups fresh or frozen peas. Cook until the liquid is absorbed and the peas are cooked. Serves 4.

GARDEN VEGETABLE CURRY

Hot and spicey describe this dish from Pakistan. The addition of yogurt at the end of cooking will tame some of the fire. Serve it with a green salad topped with citrus slices and Creamy Orange Dressing (page 15), and chilled beer.

1 tablespoon canola oil
4 cloves garlic, minced
1 tablespoon minced peeled fresh ginger
1 teaspoon red pepper flakes
1 teaspoon ground turmeric
1 teaspoon fennel seeds
1 teaspoon ground coriander
¼ teaspoon ground cumin
2 medium onions, chopped coarsely
2 medium potatoes, cut into ½-inch cubes
1 cup diced carrot
1 cup chopped red bell pepper
1 cup chopped green bell pepper
4 medium tomatoes, chopped
3 cups cauliflower florets
1 teaspoon salt
¼ cup water
2 cups fresh or frozen peas

1 cup plain nonfat yogurt
3 cups hot cooked brown rice
¼ cup chopped cilantro or parsley

In a large sauté pan over medium heat, warm the oil. Add the garlic, fresh ginger, pepper flakes, turmeric, fennel, coriander, and cumin; sauté until fragrant (about 20 seconds). Reduce the heat to low and add the onions. Cook, stirring, until soft (about 4 minutes).

Add the potatoes, carrots, bell peppers, tomatoes, cauliflower, and salt. Stir to combine; then add the water and bring to a boil, stirring constantly. Reduce the heat, cover, and simmer until the vegetables are crisp-tender (about 10 minutes). Add the peas; cover and cook until they are tender (2 to 3 minutes). Remove from the heat and stir in the yogurt.

Serve by mounding the rice and vegetables side by side; garnish with the chopped cilantro.

Serves 6 to 8.

STEWS

Although we are inclined to think of stews as hearty country fare, there are many sophisticated examples from the most elegant cuisines. Almost every cooking tradition has a selection of stews, many of which I have included. The method here is the slow cooking of a combination of ingredients, with ample time given to not only the cooking of the food but the blending of flavors.

Be sure to have a good supply of hearty bread on hand to soak up the wonderful stew juices left on the plate.

BEEF WITH TOMATOES AND RICE, CATALAN STYLE

This dish comes from the western Mediterranean corner of France. It is perfect with a mixed green salad, whole-grain French bread, and a young red wine.

2 strips turkey bacon
1 tablespoon olive oil
1 ½ pounds lean top round, all visible fat removed, cut into 1-inch cubes
1 ½ cups sliced onion
1 cup long-grain white rice
½ cup water
½ cup dry white wine
3 cups Beef Stock (page 11), or as needed
Salt, to taste
2 cups thinly sliced carrot
1 cup thinly sliced celery
¼ teaspoon freshly ground black pepper
2 large cloves garlic, crushed in a garlic press
1 teaspoon dried thyme
1 bay leaf, crumbed

1 ½ cups chopped ripe tomatoes
½ cup grated Parmesan cheese

In a heavy Dutch oven with a lid, fry the bacon over medium heat until just cooked. Drain and cut into 1-inch pieces. Set aside.

Pour off any excess fat from the pot, add the oil, and warm it over medium-high heat. Add the meat and cook it until browned. Reduce the heat to medium; stir in the onion and brown it slightly. Remove the meat and onion to a large platter.

In the oil in the same pot, add the rice and cook, stirring, over medium heat until it turns a milky color (about 3 minutes). Spoon the rice into a bowl and set aside.

Pour any remaining oil out of the pot; add the water and stir for a moment to dissolve the juices. Add the wine, stir, then return the meat and onion to the pot. Pour in the stock almost to the height of the meat and salt it lightly.

Add the carrot, celery, ground pepper, garlic, thyme, bay leaf, and reserved bacon. Bring to a simmer, cover tightly, and simmer slowly for 1 hour.

Stir in the chopped tomato and simmer until the meat is fork-tender (1 hour or more). Drain off the cooking liquid into a measuring cup and add stock or water to make 2 ½ cups. Return this liquid to the pot and bring to a boil. Stir in the reserved rice, cover, and simmer for about 20 minutes without stirring. The rice should be tender and have absorbed almost all the liquid. Taste and correct the seasoning. Just before serving, fold in the grated cheese. Serve from the casserole.

Serves 6.

Variation

Beef and Bean Stew, Arabian Style. Omit the celery and cheese. Stir in 2 cups cooked navy beans and ¼ teaspoon ground cinnamon with the tomato. Serves 8.

EASY BEEF STEW, ITALIAN STYLE

This adaptation of a popular beef stew (called Manzo brasato *in Italy) combines the traditional vegetables, which are easily prepared in a food processor for a* soffritto, *a mixture of chopped vegetables cooked in oil and reduced to a thick, glazed sauce. Serve this dish with a salad of sliced raw mushrooms and green onion tops on a bed of greens, dressed with garlic, lemon, and olive oil, and Simple Garlic Bread (page 18).*

All-purpose flour, for dusting meat
1 pound lean top round, all visible fat
removed, cut into 1-inch cubes
1 tablespoon olive oil
1 tablespoon Italian Herb Blend (page 16)
1 large clove garlic, minced
½ teaspoon salt
½ teaspoon freshly ground black pepper
½ cup coarsely chopped onion
½ cup coarsely chopped carrot
½ cup coarsely chopped celery
¼ cup dry red wine
2 cups Beef Stock (page 11)

3 medium potatoes, halved lengthwise,
then sliced
1 can (28 ounces) tomatoes, coarsely
chopped, with juice
1 bay leaf

Sprinkle the flour over the meat. In a heavy Dutch oven with a lid, warm the oil over medium-high heat. Add the beef and cook until it is brown and crusty on all sides. Remove to a plate and set aside.

Add the herb blend, garlic, salt, and ground pepper to the pot; cook for several minutes. Add the onion, carrot, and celery; cook, stirring, until the vegetables soften and become thick and slightly glazed (about 8 minutes). This is the *soffritto.*

Reduce the heat to medium-low; add the wine and stir to deglaze the pot. Add the stock, reserved beef, potatoes, tomatoes, and bay leaf. Increase the heat to high and bring the stew to a boil, then reduce the heat to low, cover the pot tightly, and simmer until the meat is tender (about 2 hours). Discard the bay leaf and serve.

Serves 4.

Variations

Ragoût de Boeuf Bordelaise. Substitute 1 teaspoon dried thyme and ¼ teaspoon ground cloves for the Italian Herb Blend.

Omit the celery. Fifteen minutes before serving, add 12 fresh mushrooms, sliced and sautéed, and 1 cup peas. Heat thoroughly.

Beef Stew, Pizza Style. Omit the potatoes. About 15 minutes before serving, sprinkle 2 ounces shredded part-skim mozzarella cheese over the top. Cover and cook until the cheese has melted. Serve over hot cooked pasta or brown rice.

CHILI CON CARNE

This dish of well-seasoned beef with chilies is one of the most famous dishes of Texas, although it is found all over the United States in different forms. Recipes are available for chili with chicken (see the variation below) and for vegetarian versions, that is, without carne (pages 104–105). This adaptation with lots of vegetables is an easy dish, hearty and very well flavored. You can vary the amount of heat by adjusting the amount (and strength) of the chili powder and fresh chopped chilies. This dish is traditionally served with steamed white rice and chilled beer.

1 pound lean ground beef
1 cup chopped onion
2 cloves garlic, minced
3 cups water
2 cups thinly sliced zucchini
2 cups sliced fresh mushrooms
¾ cup thinly sliced carrot
½ cup chopped green bell pepper
1 can (4 ounces) chopped green chilies, undrained

⅓ cup Crushed Tomatoes (page 14) or tomato paste
1 ½ tablespoons chili powder
½ teaspoon salt
1/ teaspoon dried oregano
½ teaspoon ground cumin
¼ teaspoon freshly ground black pepper
1 can (28 ounces) tomatoes, chopped, with juice
1 can (19 ounces) red kidney beans, rinsed and drained

In a large Dutch oven over medium heat, cook the meat with the onion and garlic until browned, stirring to crumble. Lift it out onto a plate and pat dry with a paper towel. Wipe the drippings from the pan.

Return the meat to the pan. Add the remaining ingredients and bring to a boil. Reduce the heat and simmer, uncovered, for 1 hour, stirring occasionally. Serve steaming hot.

Serves 8.

LEMONY VEAL STEW

This elegant version of a German Kalbsragout *would be served with a* Kopfsalat, *that is, whole Boston lettuce leaves with Light Herb Dressing (page 15), and a chilled medium-dry white wine.*

1 ½ pounds boneless veal, all visible fat
    removed, cut into 1-inch cubes
All-purpose flour, for dredging the meat
½ teaspoon salt
½ teaspoon freshly ground white pepper
1 tablespoon canola oil
2 large carrots, diced
2 large onions, chopped
Butter, if needed
½ teaspoon dried winter savory
4 medium potatoes, in small cubes
2 cups cut green beans (1-inch pieces)
2 teaspoons grated lemon zest
Juice of 2 lemons
Pinch ground nutmeg

Pat the veal cubes dry, then dredge them in the flour seasoned with the salt and ground pepper. In a stovetop casserole with a lid, warm the oil over medium heat. Sauté the carrots and onions for 5 minutes. Push them aside, add the floured veal cubes, and brown on all sides, adding a bit of butter if needed.

Sprinkle the savory over the veal and add enough water to show through the top of the stew. Cover and cook very slowly for 1 ½ hours. Add the potatoes and beans and continue to cook slowly until the vegetables are tender (about 20 minutes), adding more water during the cooking if needed. Stir in the lemon zest, lemon juice, and nutmeg and heat thoroughly. Serve hot.

Serves 6.

SLENDER BLANQUETTE DE VEAU

I can remember eating Blanquette de veau *as a student in Paris. It was very rich, with a cream sauce fortified with egg yolks. Here is a low-fat adaptation for today's palate. This dish, traditionally served with egg noodles or white rice, is more appealing with brown rice, which adds flavor and color. Serve the stew with a salad and Light Herb Dressing (page 15) and, of course, French bread.*

1 teaspoon butter
1 teaspoon canola oil
2 pounds lean boneless veal, all visible fat
    removed, cut into 1-inch cubes
3 bay leaves
2 teaspoons celery salt
1 teaspoon dried thyme
½ teaspoon freshly ground white pepper
2 cups Chicken Stock (page 11)
1 ½ pounds small white onions
½ pound fresh mushrooms, sliced
1 cup fresh or frozen tiny peas
¼ cup evaporated skimmed milk
3 tablespoons chopped parsley
3 cups hot cooked long-grain brown rice

In a heavy Dutch oven over medium heat, melt the butter and oil. Sauté the veal until lightly browned. Combine the bay leaves, celery salt, thyme, ground pepper, and stock. Pour over the veal. Reduce the heat to the lowest setting, cover, and simmer for 1 hour.

Skim off any scum that has formed. Place the onions on top of the meat. Cover and simmer until the veal and onions are tender (about 45 minutes). Stir in the mushrooms, peas, and evaporated milk. Cover and simmer for 10 minutes. Discard the bay leaves. Sprinkle with the parsley and serve over the hot rice.

Serves 6.

Variation

Veal in Wine. Substitute ¼ cup dry sherry for the evaporated milk, adding it with the onions.

URUGUAYAN CARBONADA

Here is an unusual combination of wholesome ingredients, especially the yellow vegetables. Serve this with plenty of hearty whole wheat bread to soak up the sauce and well-chilled beer.

1 tablespoon canola oil
2 large cloves garlic, chopped
1 medium onion, chopped
1 pound boneless veal, all visible fat
    removed, cut into 1-inch cubes
2 tomatoes, cubed
1 medium potato, diced
1 hubbard or butternut squash, peeled,
    seeds removed, and diced
1 medium to large sweet potato, peeled
    and diced
1 cup fresh corn kernels, cut from the cob
1 teaspoon dried thyme
1 teaspoon dried summer savory
½ teaspoon salt
½ teaspoon freshly ground white pepper

3 cups Root Vegetable Stock (page 13), or
    more if needed
1 cup long-grain white rice
2 small tart apples, cored and diced

In a heavy Dutch oven or flameproof casserole with a lid, warm the oil over medium heat. Sauté the garlic and onion until lightly browned. Add the veal and brown it.

Add the tomatoes, potato, squash, sweet potato, corn, thyme, savory, salt, ground pepper, and stock. Bring to a boil; then reduce the heat, cover, and simmer until almost done (1 ½ hours).

Add the rice and apples and simmer, covered, until the rice is cooked (about 30 minutes). Add more stock if necessary; the consistency should be slightly less liquid than a thick soup. Serve hot.

Serves 6.

CASSOULET, SLENDER STYLE

The traditional version of this dish takes several days to cook and calls for goose breast, not to mention pork rind, loin, and sausage. This adaptation takes less time and eliminates many of the fat-filled ingredients, yet almost all the flavor and special qualities of the dish remain. Keep in mind that the beans must soak overnight, and that the dish is eaten on the second day. Serve it with a green salad (try fresh green beans, slightly cooked, on a bed of mixed greens), hearty red wine or chilled beer, and lots of whole-grain French bread.

½ **pound dried navy beans**
4 **slices turkey bacon**
1 **pound lean stewing lamb, all visible fat removed, cut into 1-inch cubes or 2 cups leftover roast lamb**
¼ **pound mild Italian turkey sausage, cut into small pieces**
1 **large onion, chopped**
1 **large clove garlic, sliced thin**
2 **cups chopped tomato or 1 can (16 ounces) whole tomatoes, chopped, with juice**

1 **bay leaf**
½ **teaspoon dried thyme**
½ **teaspoon dried basil**
½ **teaspoon salt**
½ **teaspoon freshly ground black pepper**
3 **cups hot cooked long-grain brown rice**

Pour boiling water over the beans and let them soak overnight. Drain; then pour fresh water over to cover and simmer until done (about 1 hour). Drain, reserving the liquid, and set aside.

In a large stovetop casserole, fry the bacon until crisp. Drain on paper towels, crumble, and set aside.

Drain the fat from the casserole and sauté the lamb until browned. Add the lamb to the beans. Sauté the sausage, onion, and garlic until browned. Drain off the fat. Then add the tomato, bay leaf, thyme, and basil and stir well. Season with the salt and ground pepper and cook for about 1 hour, adding some of the bean liquid, if necessary. Mix in the reserved lamb, cooked beans, and bacon. Chill overnight.

The next day, add the remaining bean liquid to the casserole and cook the cassoulet slowly, for 3 to 4 hours, over low heat. Serve over the rice.

Serves 4 to 6.

LAMB AND POTATOES, PROVENÇAL STYLE

This stew—a favorite lamb dish—is infinitely quicker and easier than a cassoulet, and equally good. Serve it with mixed greens and Light Herb Dressing (page 15) and hearty red wine.

1 tablespoon olive oil
1 pound stewing lamb, all visible fat removed, cut into small chunks
2 large onions, sliced
2 cloves garlic, chopped
3 teaspoons Herbes de Provence (page 16) *or* **2 teaspoons dried basil, divided**
½ teaspoon salt, divided
½ teaspoon freshly ground black pepper
3 medium potatoes, halved lengthwise, then sliced thin
¼ cup water
4 small zucchini, sliced thin
3 cups chopped tomato

In a large stovetop casserole with a lid, warm the oil over medium-high heat. Brown the lamb thoroughly. Reduce the heat to medium, add the onions and garlic, and sauté until soft. Stir in 2 teaspoons of the herbs, ¼ teaspoon of the salt, the ground pepper, potatoes, and the water. Reduce the heat to low, cover, and cook for 20 minutes.

Stir in the zucchini and tomato with the remaining herbs and salt. Cook, stirring occasionally, until the zucchini are translucent and the potatoes are done.

Serves 6.

Variation

Lahem Mashwe. For this Middle Eastern stew, add 3 medium carrots and 3 stalks celery, both sliced thin, along with the potatoes. Instead of the herbs, use 1 teaspoon cumin seeds and 1 tablespoon chopped cilantro. Serves 6 to 8.

NEW ENGLAND PORK AND APPLESAUCE

This delicious autumn meal provides the pork and applesauce all in one dish. Serve with Triple Wheat Biscuits (page 17) and chilled medium-dry white wine.

2 pounds boneless pork tenderloin, all visible fat removed, cut into chunks
3 cups homemade applesauce, slightly sweetened
¼ cup water
¼ cup apple cider vinegar *or* dry white wine
1 tablespoon ground cinnamon
2 teaspoons ground nutmeg
1 teaspoon ground cloves
8 small red potatoes, cut into quarters
6 carrots, cut into chunks
2 stalks celery, sliced diagonally
2 cups white pearl onions
2 firm tart apples, cored and sliced thin

In a large Dutch oven over medium heat, combine the pork, applesauce, water, wine, and spices. Cover tightly and cook for 15 minutes. Reduce the heat.

Add the potatoes, carrots, celery, and onions, and simmer about 1 ½ hours. Fifteen minutes before serving, add the apple slices.

Serves 6.

Variation

Cranberry-Applesauce Pork. Combine 1 cup whole cranberry sauce, ¼ cup apricot preserves, and ¼ cup cranberry juice; add with the vegetables. If desired, instead of the new red potatoes substitute 4 large sweet potatoes, peeled, halved, and sliced thick.

Moroccan Bean Stew

Called Dfina, *this stew is one of many possible lamb and bean combinations and a favorite in Mediterranean and Middle Eastern cooking. The stew will take some time to prepare (note that the chickpeas and lima beans must soak overnight), but it will fill your kitchen with a wonderful aroma. Serve it with a salad of oranges and red onion slices on greens, garnished with chopped fresh mint, and hearty wheat bread or pita.*

½ **pound dried chickpeas**
½ **pound dried baby lima beans**
2 **tablespoons olive oil**
2 **large onions, chopped fine**
1 ½ **pounds lean stewing lamb, all visible fat removed, cut into chunks**
1 **teaspoon ground coriander**
1 **teaspoon ground cumin**
⅛ **teaspoon ground saffron**
24 **small new potatoes**
2 **large carrots, cut into 2-inch pieces**
6 **cups water**
Juice of 1 lemon

Salt and freshly ground black pepper, to taste
2 **tablespoons slivered almonds, toasted**
2 **tablespoons chopped fresh mint**

Measure the chickpeas and lima beans into a large bowl, add boiling water to 2 inches above the beans, and soak overnight. Drain and rinse. Set aside.

In a heavy Dutch oven over medium-high heat, warm the oil. Add the onions and sauté until golden. Combine with the chickpeas and beans.

Add the lamb to the pot and sauté until lightly browned. Stir in the coriander, cumin, and saffron; let the spices sizzle for a minute. Then stir in the reserved chickpeas, beans, and onions. Tuck the potatoes and carrots around the other ingredients. Add the water and bring to a simmer. Skim the surface; then cover and place over the lowest heat for 1 ½ to 2 hours. Stir in the lemon juice and taste. Add the salt and pepper to taste.

Continue to simmer until the liquid has been mostly absorbed (about 2 hours). Sprinkle with the toasted nuts and chopped mint. Serve hot.

Serves 8.

Cajun Red Beans and Rice

This zesty bean and rice stew is easily made, but note that the beans must soak overnight. By omitting the ham or bacon, this recipe, as well as the variations, make superb vegetarian fare; adjust the seasoning accordingly. Serve with hot Skinny Corn Bread (page 17) and chilled beer.

1 pound dried red kidney beans, rinsed and sorted
2 large onions, chopped
1 green bell pepper, chopped
1 cup chopped celery
1 cup minced smoked turkey ham (about ¼ pound)
1 teaspoon Cajun Pepper Mix (page 17)
1 ½ cups long-grain brown rice

3 green onions, sliced thin, tops included
3 tablespoons minced parsley

Place the beans in a large heavy kettle, pour in 2 quarts boiling water, cover, and soak overnight.

Drain the beans well. Stir in 11 cups water, the onions, bell pepper, celery, ham, pepper mix, and rice. Bring to a boil over high heat, then reduce the heat to low, so that the liquid simmers. Cover and cook for 2 ½ hours.

Stir in the green onions and parsley and cook, uncovered, on the lowest setting until most of the liquid is absorbed (about 30 minutes). Serve hot.

Serves 8.

Variations

Red Beans, Dominican Style. Substitute 2 cups small red beans (adzuki beans) for the kidney beans. Substitute 4 strips turkey bacon, fried, drained, and cut into pieces, for the ham. Omit the pepper mix and add 2 tomatoes, chopped; 1 teaspoon dried oregano; and ½ jalapeño pepper, minced. Cook for about 2 hours in all. Garnish with chopped cilantro.

Black Beans and Rice, Cuban Style. Substitute 1 pound dried black beans for the kidney beans. Substitute 2 slices turkey bacon, fried, drained, and cut into pieces, for the ham. Omit the pepper mix and add 2 large cloves garlic, minced; 1 small red chile, minced; 1 tablespoon red wine vinegar; ½ teaspoon dried cumin; and ⅛ teaspoon cayenne pepper. Cook for about 3 hours in all. Garnish with chopped cilantro rather than the parsley.

Feijoada

This unusual stew is considered the national dish of Brazil. Serve it with palm hearts and avocado slices on a bed of greens. If you prefer, you can omit the oranges.

2 cups dried black beans, rinsed and
    sorted
1 cup long-grain brown rice
½ teaspoon salt
1 bay leaf
1 tablespoon olive oil
4 cups chopped onion
3 large cloves garlic, minced
½ pound smoked turkey sausage, cut into
    ½-inch pieces
1 pound tomatoes, chopped (about 2 cups)
¼ teaspoon ground cumin
⅛ teaspoon crushed red pepper flakes
2 large oranges, peeled and chopped
    (optional)
¼ cup chopped parsley
1 teaspoon grated orange zest
⅓ cup farina or wheat germ, toasted

Place the beans in a large Dutch oven. Cover with boiling water 2 inches above the beans and cook over high heat for 2 minutes. Remove from heat and let stand, covered, for 1 hour.

Drain the beans. Add 7 cups water, the rice, salt, and bay leaf. Bring to a boil, cover, reduce the heat, and simmer until the beans are tender (about 3 hours). Set aside but keep warm.

In a large skillet over medium-high heat, sauté the onion and garlic in oil until tender (about 5 minutes). Add the sausage, tomatoes, cumin, and red pepper flakes and cook for 2 minutes.

Stir the tomato mixture into the reserved bean mixture and cook, uncovered, for 30 minutes. Top with the chopped oranges, parsley, and orange zest. Sprinkle with the toasted farina and serve.

Serves 8.

THREE GRAINS AND HAM

This variation on an Indian dish called Keyma *takes some time to cook (note that the barley must soak overnight) but is very satisfying. Serve it with fresh green beans and sliced radishes on a bed of greens with Light Herb Dressing (page 15) and whole wheat bread.*

½ cup hulled barley
2 tablespoons olive oil
2 ounces turkey ham, cut into ½-inch dice
3 large cloves garlic, sliced
1 large red onion, chopped
5 medium green onions, tops included, sliced
¼ cup wild rice
4 cups Chicken Stock (page 11), divided
1 teaspoon dried oregano
½ cup lentils, rinsed
¼ cup bulgur
¼ cup firmly packed chopped parsley
Salt and freshly ground black pepper, to taste

Soak the barley in 2 ½ cups water overnight.

In a large Dutch oven over medium heat, warm the oil. Sauté the ham, garlic, red onion, and green onions until soft (about 5 minutes). Add the rice, 2 cups of the stock, 1 cup water, and the oregano. Bring to a boil, then reduce the heat, cover, and simmer for 30 minutes.

Drain the barley and add it to the pot along with the lentils, bulgur, and remaining 2 cups stock. Cover and simmer until the grains are tender (about 40 minutes). Uncover and simmer until the liquid evaporates (about 10 minutes). Stir in the parsley. Add salt and freshly ground black pepper to taste. Serve immediately.

Serves 6.

Chicken Cacciatore

This chicken and vegetable combination is a popular Italian dish, best made with fresh tomatoes. Accompany it with steamed broccoli and young green beans, marinated, served at room temperature (see page 16), plus chunks of crusty Italian bread and dry white wine.

2 tablespoons olive oil

1 broiler-fryer chicken (about 3 pounds), cut into pieces

½ cup thinly sliced onion

2 cloves garlic, minced or pressed

½ pound fresh mushrooms, sliced thin

1 large green bell pepper, cut into strips

1 medium carrot, cut into very thin disks

4 cups chopped fresh Italian plum tomatoes or canned tomatoes, with juice

2 teaspoons Italian Herb Blend (page 16) *or* ½ teaspoon each dried basil, oregano, thyme, and marjoram

½ teaspoon salt

½ teaspoon freshly ground black pepper

½ cup Chicken Stock (page 11) or water

½ cup dry white wine

8 to 10 ounces whole wheat or semolina spaghetti

Parmesan cheese, for sprinkling (optional)

In a large skillet or Dutch oven with a lid, heat the oil over medium-high heat. Sauté the chicken pieces until golden brown. Set aside on a platter and sauté the onion and garlic until slightly browned.

Return the chicken to the pot and add the mushrooms, bell pepper, carrot, tomatoes, herb blend, salt, ground pepper, stock, and wine. Cover and simmer for about 1 hour. Remove the cover to let the sauce reduce somewhat and continue cooking until the chicken is very tender.

Cook the spaghetti (see page 21). Drain and transfer to a serving bowl.

Remove the skin from the chicken pieces. Arrange the chicken, vegetables, and sauce over the hot spaghetti. Sprinkle with the Parmesan cheese, if desired. Serve at once.

Serves 6.

Note: If you have leftovers from this meal, remove the chicken from the bones and mince it. Add 2 inches mild Italian turkey sausage (cut into small pieces, fried, and drained) to the sauce and serve over freshly cooked spinach noodles or vegetable spirals.

Variation

Turkey Cacciatore. Substitute 4 cups cooked turkey (as much white meat as possible) for the chicken pieces. Cook about 1 hour in all.

CHICKEN PAPRIKA

Adding mushrooms and peppers to the Austrian Paprikahendl *is an adaptation of a recipe that comes from a Viennese friend. An elegant dish, it is traditionally served with noodles or steaming rice. Add a salad of soft head lettuce (Boston or buttercrunch) with Light Herb Dressing (page 15) and crisp dry white wine.*

1 tablespoon canola oil
1 broiler-fryer chicken (about 3 pounds),
   cut into pieces
2 large onions, chopped
2 tablespoons sweet Hungarian paprika
1 tablespoon all-purpose flour
½ teaspoon salt
½ teaspoon freshly ground white pepper
1 can (8 ounces) whole tomatoes,
   chopped, with juice
¼ pound fresh mushrooms, sliced
½ green bell pepper, sliced
1 pound egg noodles
½ cup buttermilk

In a large Dutch oven with a lid, heat the oil over medium-high heat. Sauté the chicken pieces until slightly browned. Remove to a plate and set aside.

Reduce the heat to medium, add the onions, and sauté slowly until they are soft and golden. Stir in the paprika, flour, salt, ground pepper, and tomatoes. Stir well. Add the reserved chicken pieces, mushrooms, and bell pepper. Cover and simmer gently for about 45 minutes.

Cook the noodles in lightly salted water. Drain, then place on a heated platter. Arrange the chicken pieces on top and keep warm. Stir the buttermilk into the sauce and vegetables, heat thoroughly, and pour over the chicken. Serve immediately.

Serves 8.

Variation

Chicken Paprika with Dumplings. Omit the tomatoes and noodles. Add 1 cup Chicken Stock (page 11) with the chicken pieces. Cook the chicken for about 30 minutes; during that time prepare the dough for Parsley Dumplings (page 17). Stir the buttermilk into the sauce and bring to a boil. Drop the dumpling dough in 8 mounds on the simmering liquid. Reduce the heat, cover tightly, and cook for 20 minutes. Do not lift the lid to peek while the dumplings cook. Serve from the pot.

BRUNSWICK STEW

From the American South, this dish in its original form contained no vegetables and was made from squirrel. The updated version given here changes both, although I am sorely tempted to try some of those squirrels that destroy my bird feeders. On second thought, let's stick to chicken. Serve this with a tossed green salad and Skinny Corn Bread (page 17).

1 tablespoon canola oil
All-purpose flour, salt, and freshly ground
  black pepper, for sprinkling
1 stewing chicken (about 4 pounds), cut
  into pieces
2 large onions, chopped
2 large cloves garlic, minced
2 large green bell peppers, chopped
1 cup chopped celery
2 tablespoons Worcestershire sauce,
  divided
1 tablespoon sweet Hungarian paprika
1 teaspoon dried thyme
¼ cup finely chopped parsley
Generous dash red pepper flakes

8 cups peeled chunked tomato or 1 can
  (28 ounces) whole tomatoes, with juice
2 packages (10 ounces each) frozen cut
  okra
2 packages (10 ounces each) frozen lima
  beans
3 cups corn kernels, cut from the cob,
  cooked

In a large Dutch oven with a lid, warm the oil over medium-high heat. Sprinkle the flour, salt, and ground pepper over the chicken pieces, then sauté until golden. Remove them to a platter and set aside.

Pour off any fat from the pot and add the onions, garlic, bell peppers, and celery. Cook, stirring, until the vegetables soften. Add 1 tablespoon of the Worcestershire sauce, the paprika, thyme, parsley, and pepper flakes; stir well.

Purée the tomato in the food processor. Add to the stew with the okra; mix well. Return the reserved chicken pieces to the pot, cover, and simmer for 1 hour, stirring occasionally. Add the lima beans and cook 30 minutes more, skimming off any scum that rises to the top.

Remove the chicken and set aside to cool slightly. Cut it up, discarding skin and bones, and return it to the pot. Stir in the corn and the remaining 1 tablespoon Worcestershire sauce; heat thoroughly before serving.

Serves 8 to 10.

Variation

Southern Chicken Stew with Carrot Dumplings. Omit the okra and add 1 cup Chicken Stock (page 11). After you have returned the cut-up chicken to the pot and added the corn, prepare the dough for Parsley Dumplings (page 17), adding ¼-cup shredded carrot to the dough. Drop the dumplings onto the simmering liquid in 8 mounds. Cover tightly (don't peek) and cook for 15 minutes.

Arroz con Pollo

This delicious Spanish dish, which has traveled to the Caribbean and South America, is one of the best known. Serve it with a green salad, chunks of hearty bread, and light, dry red wine.

2 tablespoons olive oil
Salt and freshly ground black pepper
1 broiler-fryer chicken (about 3 pounds),
    cut into pieces
2 cloves garlic, chopped
2 medium onions, chopped
4 ounces cooked turkey ham, diced
1 green bell pepper, chopped
1 red bell pepper, cut into strips
2 medium tomatoes, chopped
1 tablespoon paprika
¼ teaspoon saffron threads, crushed in a
    mortar or ½ teaspoon ground saffron
2 ¼ cups long-grain brown rice
4 cups Chicken Stock (page 11)
1 package (10 ounces) frozen tiny peas
2 tablespoons finely chopped parsley, for
    garnish

In a heavy flameproof casserole over medium-high heat, warm the oil. Sprinkle the salt and pepper over the chicken pieces and sauté them until golden. Transfer to a plate and set aside. Then sauté the garlic, onions, ham, and bell peppers until the vegetables are soft. Add the tomatoes and cook until the mixture is thick (about 10 minutes).

Stir in the paprika and saffron, then add the rice and stock. Return the chicken pieces to the casserole. Taste and add more salt and ground pepper, if needed. Bring to a simmer, cover tightly, and cook over very low heat for 30 minutes. Stir in the peas and continue to cook, covered, until the chicken is tender and almost all the liquid has been absorbed. Don't worry if the dish seems somewhat soupy.

Remove it from the heat and let it stand, covered, for 10 minutes; the remaining liquid will be absorbed. Garnish with the parsley and serve hot.

Serves 6.

Variation

Chicken and Rice, Moroccan Style. Omit the ham and tomatoes. Sauté ½ cup slivered almonds, ½ teaspoon ground ginger, and ⅛ teaspoon turmeric with the vegetables. Reduce the paprika to 1 teaspoon. Along with the peas, stir in 2 cups cooked chickpeas and 3 tablespoons lemon juice.

EASY CHICKEN TARRAGON

This adaptation of an old French recipe is very simple and the tarragon flavors it in a special way. If you prefer, serve this dish over hot cooked rice. Be sure to save any extra stock for another time.

2 pounds chicken parts
2 cups water
1 teaspoon dried tarragon
2 carrots, cut crosswise into thirds, then quartered
2 onions, thinly sliced
1 stalk celery, sliced diagonally, with tops chopped
¼ pound mushrooms, wiped clean and sliced
¼ cup minced parsley
8 ounces linguini, plain or spinach, cooked al dente (see page 21)

In a large Dutch oven combine the chicken, water, and tarragon. Bring to a boil, reduce the heat, and simmer for 30 minutes. Add the carrots, onions, and celery and cook until the vegetables are tender, about 10 minutes. About 5 minutes before serving, stir in the mushrooms and parsley.

Remove the skin from the chicken and discard. Spoon the chicken and vegetables over the hot linguini.

Serves 6.

Note: For a quick version of this dish, substitute 1 pound boneless chicken breast, cut into strips, for the chicken parts and 1 cup Chicken Stock (page 11) for the water. Cook everything together about 15 minutes, adding the mushrooms and parsley in the last 5 minutes.

CHICKEN AND RICE, ARABIAN STYLE

This chicken and rice combination, called Kabsa, *is one of Saudi Arabia's favorite dishes and a fine illustration of the interesting flavors of this region. Serve it with a salad of thinly sliced zucchini and cucumber, topped with Light Herb Dressing (page 15), and warm whole wheat pita bread.*

2 cups long-grain white rice
2 tablespoons canola oil
2 medium onions, sliced
5 cloves garlic, crushed
1 broiler-fryer chicken (about 3 pounds), cut into pieces, all fat and skin removed
½ cup Tomato Purée (page 14)
2 medium tomatoes, chopped
3 cups hot water
2 medium carrots, grated
Grated zest of 1 orange
6 whole cloves
6 whole cardamom seeds
4 sticks cinnamon
½ teaspoon salt
½ teaspoon freshly ground white pepper
¼ cup raisins
¼ cup almonds, blanched and sliced

Cover the rice with boiling water and soak for at least 15 minutes.

In a large Dutch oven with a lid, warm the oil over medium heat. Sauté the onions and garlic until they begin to brown. Add the chicken pieces, tomato purée, and chopped tomatoes and cook over low heat, stirring, for about 5 minutes. Add the hot water, grated carrots, orange zest, cloves, cardamom, cinnamon, salt, and ground pepper. Cook over low heat for 20 to 25 minutes. Remove the chicken and keep warm.

Drain the rice and add it to the sauce. Continue cooking the sauce slowly until the rice is cooked and dry (about 15 minutes). Transfer the rice to a heated platter, arrange the reserved chicken pieces on top, and garnish with the raisins and almonds. Serve immediately.

Serves 8.

PAELLA

This colorful medley of meats, seafood, vegetables, and rice is Spain's most popular dish and makes superb party fare. Despite the varied ingredients, once everything is assembled the dish is quickly made. If you don't have a paella pan, use a 16-inch skillet or large sauté pan with a lid, or a flameproof casserole. Serve this dish with hearty whole wheat bread and light red wine.

3 pounds chicken breasts, split
Salt and freshly ground pepper, to taste
2 tablespoons olive oil
4 ounces lean pork tenderloin, chopped
4 ounces garlic-flavored turkey sausage, cut into ¼-inch slices
4 ounces turkey ham, chopped
2 medium onions, chopped fine
4 cloves garlic, chopped
2 red bell peppers, sliced
12 large shrimp, shelled (tails left on) and deveined
1 lobster tail, cut into 8 pieces
3 cups short-grain white rice
3 tablespoons chopped parsley
1 bay leaf
¼ teaspoon saffron threads, crushed in a mortar, or 1 teaspoon ground saffron
6 cups Chicken Stock (page 11)
1 cup fresh peas or 1 package (10 ounces) frozen peas, defrosted
16 clams, scrubbed
16 mussels, scrubbed
Lemon wedges, for garnish
Chopped parsley, for garnish

Season the chicken pieces with the salt and ground pepper. In a paella pan over medium-high heat, warm the oil. Sauté the chicken until golden. Transfer to a platter and keep warm.

Add the pork, sausage, and ham to the pan and cook, stirring, for about 10 minutes. Transfer to a plate and set aside. Reduce the heat to medium and add the onions, garlic, and bell peppers; sauté until the onions are soft. Add the shrimp and lobster pieces and cook just until they turn pink (no more than 3 minutes). Transfer to a plate and set aside.

Return the pork combination to the pan, then stir in the rice, parsley, bay leaf, and saffron. Pour in the stock, stir to mix, and cook, uncovered, stirring from time to time, for 10 minutes. Stir in the peas. Bury the reserved chicken pieces in the rice together with the reserved seafood. Push the clams and mussels into the rice, with the side that will open uppermost, if possible. Cover tightly and cook over the lowest heat until the rice is tender and all the liquid is absorbed.

Let stand, covered, for 10 minutes. Serve directly from the paella pan, garnished with the lemon wedges and sprinkled with the chopped parsley.

Serves 8.

TURKEY AND BACON STEW

This northeastern American stew offers a good way to use up leftover turkey from the holidays. Use as much white meat as possible and enjoy the savory blend of turkey, vegetables, and herbs. Serve it with Triple Wheat Biscuits (page 17) or Skinny Corn Bread (page 17) and a mixed salad with Sesame Dressing (page 15).

2 slices turkey bacon, diced
2 large onions, chopped
2 carrots, sliced thin
4 ribs celery, sliced in thin diagonals
¼ pound mushrooms, sliced
2 tablespoons all-purpose flour
1 tablespoon wheat germ
4 medium red potatoes, diced
1 teaspoon dried thyme
½ teaspoon rubbed dried sage
2 bay leaves
½ teaspoon salt
½ teaspoon freshly ground white pepper
2 cups Turkey Stock (page 12) or Chicken Stock (page 11)
½ cup dry white wine or dry sherry

2 cups diced cooked turkey
½ cup plain nonfat yogurt
Chopped parsley, for garnish

In a large stovetop casserole over medium heat, fry the bacon until crisp. Drain on paper towels. Drain off almost all of the fat. Sauté the onions, carrots, and celery until soft; then stir in the mushrooms and cook for 2 minutes. Add the flour and wheat germ and cook for 2 minutes longer. Stir in the potatoes.

Remove the casserole from the heat and add the thyme, sage, bay leaves, salt, ground pepper, stock, and wine. Stir well. Cook over low heat for 45 minutes. Add the turkey and reserved bacon and cook for 15 minutes. Stir in the yogurt and heat thoroughly but do not boil.

Remove from the heat, discard the bay leaves, and sprinkle each portion with the parsley. Serve hot.

Serves 6.

Salmon Jambalaya

This adaptation of a traditional Cajun dish nicely illustrates the lively flavors of Louisiana cooking. Serve it with a salad of romaine, shredded spinach, and sweet head lettuce topped with Light Herb Dressing (page 15), and chilled dry white wine.

1 tablespoon butter
1 cup chopped onion
1 cup sliced celery
1 cup coarsely chopped green bell pepper
2 cloves garlic, crushed in a garlic press
1 cup diced turkey ham
1 ½ cups long-grain white rice
½ teaspoon dried thyme
½ teaspoon Cajun Pepper Mix (page 17)
¼ teaspoon salt
¼ teaspoon freshly ground white pepper
2 cups coarsely chopped tomato

3 cups Chicken Stock (page 11)
Water, if needed
1 ½ cups flaked cooked fresh salmon

In a large skillet with a lid, melt the butter over medium heat. Sauté the onion, celery, bell pepper, and garlic until the onion is soft. Add the ham, rice, thyme, pepper mix, salt, and ground pepper. Cook, stirring, for 10 minutes. Add the chopped tomato and stock; bring to a boil and cook, uncovered, for 5 minutes.

Reduce the heat to low, cover, and simmer for 45 to 50 minutes, stirring occasionally. Add a little water if the jambalaya seems to be getting too dry. Add the salmon and cook until heated through (about 5 minutes). Serve at once.

Serves 6.

SOUTHWEST SEAFOOD STEW

This hearty and nourishing stew combines the strong, hot flavors of the American Southwest with the colors and textures of fresh vegetables, legumes, and different kinds of seafood. It is easily made. Serve it with Skinny Corn Bread (page 17) or toasted corn tortillas, and chilled beer.

2 tablespoons olive oil, divided
2 medium zucchini, cut in half lengthwise, then sliced
2 medium onions, chopped coarsely
4 cloves garlic, minced
1 large red bell pepper, diced
1 large yellow or green bell pepper, diced
1 small jalapeño pepper, seeded and diced
1 can (28 ounces) plum tomatoes, chopped, with juice
5 medium fresh tomatoes, chopped coarsely
½ pound fresh mushrooms, sliced
1 tablespoon dried basil
1 tablespoon dried oregano
1 tablespoon chili powder
2 teaspoons ground cumin

1 teaspoon freshly ground black pepper
1 teaspoon fennel seeds
½ cup chopped cilantro or flat-leaf (Italian) parsley
1 cup cooked kidney beans, drained
1 cup cooked chickpeas, drained
1 pound cooked seafood mixture, such as medium shrimp, crabmeat, scallops, tuna, and lobster tail
2 tablespoons fresh lemon juice
4 cups hot cooked long-grain white rice
Shredded reduced-fat Monterey jack cheese, for garnish

In a large heavy Dutch oven over medium heat, warm 1 tablespoon of the oil. Sauté the zucchini until just tender. With a slotted spoon remove it to a plate and set aside.

Add the remaining 1 tablespoon oil to the pot. Sauté the onions, garlic, bell peppers, and jalapeño pepper until tender (about 8 minutes).

Reduce the heat to low and stir in the reserved zucchini, the canned and fresh tomatoes, mushrooms, basil, oregano, chili powder, cumin, ground pepper, fennel seeds, and cilantro. Cook, uncovered and stirring often, for 30 minutes. Stir in the beans and chickpeas and cook for 10 minutes more. Add the seafood mixture and cook until it is heated through. Stir in the lemon juice.

Serve the stew over the rice and sprinkle the shredded cheese over each portion.

Serves 8.

MEDITERRANEAN TROUT STEW

This simple combination of fish and rice makes an easy and delicate supper dish. Serve it with crusty whole-grain bread to soak up the juices.

1 tablespoon olive oil
1 cup long-grain brown rice
1 cup chopped celery
1 cup chopped onion
½ cup minced watercress *or* chopped green bell pepper
3 cloves garlic, minced
½ teaspoon sweet Hungarian paprika
½ teaspoon dried thyme
2 cups Fish Stock (page 12)
1 pound trout fillets
1 cup chopped peeled Italian plum tomatoes
1 package (10 ounces) frozen tiny peas, defrosted

In a stovetop casserole over medium heat, warm the oil. Sauté the rice, celery, onion, watercress, garlic, paprika, and thyme, stirring constantly, until the mixture is fragrant (3 to 4 minutes).

Add the stock, increase the heat to high, and bring to a boil. Reduce the heat to low, cover, and simmer, until the rice is almost cooked (about 40 minutes). Add the fish, cover, and simmer for 10 minutes. Break it up into chunks, and stir in the tomatoes and peas. Cover and simmer until completely heated through. Serve hot.

Serves 4.

Variation

Monkfish, Mediterranean Style. Instead of the trout, use 1 pound monkfish fillets, skinned and cut into 1-inch slices. Substitute 2 red bell peppers, cut into strips, for the watercress. Garnish with lemon slices.

FISHERMAN'S STEW, PORTUGUESE STYLE

This dish, called Caldeirada a pescadora *in Portugal, is a delicious stew with very simple ingredients. Serve it from the casserole with crusty bread and dry white wine.*

1 tablespoon olive oil
4 onions, sliced
3 large cloves garlic, minced
1 green bell pepper, chopped
1 red bell pepper, chopped
¼ cup chopped parsley
1 teaspoon coriander seeds
2 pounds mixed fish, such as haddock,
    cod, or sea bass, cut into bite-size
    pieces
5 medium tomatoes, peeled and chopped,
    or 2 cups chopped canned tomatoes,
    with juice
6 medium potatoes, halved lengthwise,
    then sliced
1 bay leaf
1 teaspoon salt
½ teaspoon freshly ground white pepper
1 cup dry white wine

In a deep stovetop casserole with a lid, warm the oil over medium heat. Sauté the onions, garlic, bell pepper, parsley, and coriander seeds until the onions are golden. Stir in the fish, tomatoes, potatoes, bay leaf, salt, ground pepper, and wine. Add just enough water to cover. Cover the casserole and simmer for about 45 minutes. Remove from the heat, discard the bay leaf, and serve at once.

Serves 6 to 8.

Variation

Mussel Stew, Mediterranean Style. Sauté ¼ pound sliced fresh mushrooms with the onions and garlic. Substitute 4 pounds mussels, well scrubbed and debearded, for the fish; add them after the stew has cooked for about 30 minutes.

Lentils, Monastery Style

An adaptation of a popular Spanish soup, this dish is an all-time favorite in my house. It is simple, unusual, and delicious. Serve it with a mixed green salad or slightly cooked, marinated vegetables, such as green beans, broccoli, and bell peppers. Chilled beer or dry white wine go well with the dish. Don't forget chunks of hearty bread to soak up the juices.

2 tablespoons olive oil
2 large onions, chopped
2 large carrots, chopped or sliced thin
2 medium potatoes, cut into 1-inch cubes
1 teaspoon dried thyme
½ teaspoon dried marjoram
3 cups Vegetable Stock (page 12)
1 cup lentils, rinsed
¼ cup chopped parsley
1 can (28 ounces) tomatoes, chopped, with juice
½ teaspoon salt, or to taste
¼ cup dry sherry (optional)
2 tablespoons shredded reduced-fat sharp Cheddar cheese

In a stovetop casserole over medium heat, warm the oil. Sauté the onions, carrots, and potatoes for about 5 minutes. Add the thyme and marjoram and sauté for 1 minute longer.

Reduce the heat to low and stir in the stock, lentils, parsley, and tomatoes. Add the salt and cook, covered, for about 45 minutes. Stir in the sherry, if desired.

To serve, sprinkle the cheese on top of each portion.

Serves 4 to 6.

Note: For a quick version of this dish, cover the lentils with boiling water, and presoak for six hours. Drain, rinse well, and add to the casserole. Slice the potatoes thinly and use 2 cups of stock. Reduce cooking time from 45 to 20 minutes.

Variations

Lentil-eggplant Stew, Sicilian Style. Sauté 3 cloves garlic, minced, with the other vegetables. With the addition of the stock and other ingredients, stir in 1 small eggplant, peeled and cut into ½-inch cubes, and ¼ cup dry red wine. Omit the sherry. Cook as above.

Serves 6.

Lentils and Rice. For this variation of a Middle Eastern dish called *Mujaddara*, omit the potatoes, tomatoes, sherry, and cheese. Add 5 cups water and ¾ cup long-grain brown rice. Simmer until the rice is tender. Taste and adjust the seasoning, then simmer, uncovered, until the liquid is absorbed. The *Mujaddara* is usually cooked ahead of time and eaten at room temperature.

MOROCCAN SPICY VEGETABLE STEW

For an authentic rendition of this recipe, you should prepare the couscous as indicated below, allowing about 1 hour cooking time. Yes, you can buy it in a box, and it cooks up very quickly, but it can be tasteless and gluey. If possible, buy the couscous in bulk at the natural foods store and enjoy the savory smells of this dish as everything cooks slowly. Serve this stew with chunks of hearty whole wheat bread and a lightly minted tea.

1 cup couscous
3 tablespoons olive oil, divided
½ cup cold water
1 large onion, chopped
1 large green bell pepper, chopped
1 large red bell pepper, chopped
2 carrots, sliced thin
1 cup chopped tomato or 1 can (8 ounces) whole tomatoes, chopped, with juice
1 cup Vegetable Stock (page 12)
1 tablespoon lemon juice
1 teaspoon ground coriander
½ teaspoon ground cinnamon

½ teaspoon saffron threads, crushed, or ¼ teaspoon ground saffron
¾ teaspoon salt, divided
2 cups cooked chickpeas, drained, or 1 can (15 ounces) chickpeas, rinsed and drained
1 medium zucchini, quartered lengthwise, then sliced
½ cup hot water
Toasted sesame seeds, for garnish
Hot Pepper Sauce (page 15; see Note)

To prepare the couscous, combine it with 1 tablespoon of the oil, stir well, and pour into the steam pan of a couscousière or a shallow colander that fits inside a stovetop casserole or Dutch oven with a tight-fitting lid. If the holes in the colander are too large, line it with dampened cheesecloth. Steam the couscous over simmering water or stock for 20 minutes. Transfer the couscous to a bowl and stir in ½ cup cold water, breaking up all the lumps with a fork. Return the couscous to the steam pan or colander.

Meanwhile, in a large stovetop casserole or Dutch oven with a tight-fitting lid, warm the remaining 2 tablespoons oil. Sauté the onion over medium heat until softened; then add the bell peppers and carrots and cook for 5 minutes. Stir in the tomato, stock, lemon juice, coriander, cinnamon, saffron, and ½ teaspoon of the salt. Mix well.

Place the couscous container on top of the casserole, cover, and simmer for 15 minutes. Uncover. Stir the chickpeas and zucchini into the vegetable mixture. Return the couscous to a bowl and stir in the remaining ¼ teaspoon salt and the ½ cup hot water. Return the couscous mixture to the steam pan, replace the pan over the vegetable mixture, cover, and simmer for 10 to 15 minutes.

Fluff up the couscous with a fork. Spoon it around the edges of a large, deep platter and arrange the vegetables in the center. Sprinkle the sesame seeds over the top.

Pass the Hot Pepper Sauce.

Serves 6.

Note: If you prefer, omit the Hot Pepper Sauce and add ¼ teaspoon ground cumin and ¼ teaspoon red pepper flakes with the coriander and cinnamon.

Rishtayeh

This Syrian dish is an unusual yet simple combination of ingredients. An interesting accompaniment would be tomatoes stuffed with a mixture of rice, currants, pine nuts, and chopped mint, then baked.

1 cup lentils, rinsed
6 cups water
1 tablespoon olive oil
2 medium onions, sliced
1 large clove garlic, minced
1 cup minced parsley
1 package (10 ounces) fresh spinach, stems removed, leaves chopped, or 1 package (10 ounces) frozen chopped spinach
2 cups flat noodles, spirals, or elbow macaroni
Salt, to taste

In a large stovetop casserole, combine the lentils and the water. Bring to a boil, then simmer until the lentils are tender (45 to 60 minutes).

In a medium skillet over medium heat, warm the oil. Sauté the onions, garlic, and parsley until the onions are soft. Add to the cooked lentils and their liquid.

Stir the spinach and noodles into the casserole. Taste and add salt, if necessary. Let simmer until the noodles are cooked (about 10 minutes), adding water if necessary. Serve hot.

Serves 8.

Note: For a quicker meal, cover the lentils with boiling water in the morning and allow them to soak until mealtime. Drain, rinse well, and then cook them with only 4 cups of water until the onion mixture is ready. Combine everything, add the spinach and noodles, and proceed as above.

WINTER VEGETABLE STEW

This stew is even better served the next day.

1 tablespoon olive oil
1 medium yellow onion, thinly sliced
½ red onion, thinly sliced
2 cloves garlic, crushed
1 leek, chopped
2 celery stalks, including tops, coarsely
    chopped
¼ cup chopped fresh parsley
2 teaspoons dried oregano
1 teaspoon dried rosemary
1 teaspoon whole fennel seed
1 bay leaf
1 large potato, chopped
1 turnip, peeled and chopped
2 large carrots, scraped and chopped
½ pound winter squash (butternut,
    acorn), rind and seeds removed,
    chopped
1 can (16 ounces) tomatoes, coarsely
    chopped, with juice
2 cups cooked chickpeas or soybeans

4 cups Vegetable Stock or Root Vegetable
    Stock (page 12)
¾ cup small whole wheat pasta

In a large stovetop casserole, heat the oil. Add the onions, garlic, leek, and celery and sauté over medium heat until they soften, about 10 minutes. Add the herbs and stir well to blend. Stir in the remaining ingredients, except the pasta. Bring to a boil, reduce the heat to low, cover, and simmer, stirring from time to time, for 2 hours.

In the meantime prepare Creamy Pesto by combining ½ cup Yogurt Cheese (page 16) and ¼ cup Pesto (page 15). Refrigerate until ready to use. About 15 minutes before the stew is done, cook the pasta al dente (see page 21), drain it well, and stir into the stew. Season the dish with salt and pepper.

Spoon the Creamy Pesto over each portion and serve.

Serves 4 to 6.

VEGETARIAN CHILI

This wonderful dish takes a while to cook, but it is hearty and delicious. Serve it with a salad of romaine and orange slices with Creamy Orange Dressing (page 15), and lots of Skinny Corn Bread (page 17).

2 ½ cups dried kidney beans
6 cups boiling water
1 teaspoon salt, divided
1 cup medium-grain bulgur
1 cup tomato juice
1 tablespoon canola oil
3 medium onions, chopped
4 cloves garlic, minced
1 cup chopped celery
1 cup chopped carrot
1 cup chopped green bell pepper
2 teaspoons minced jalapeño pepper
2 teaspoons chili powder
Juice of ½ lemon
1 teaspoon ground cumin
1 teaspoon dried basil
2 cups chopped tomato
¼ cup dry red wine
Dash cayenne pepper
¼ cup chopped cilantro or parsley
½ cup plain nonfat yogurt

Place the kidney beans in a large pot, cover with the boiling water, and soak for 6 hours. Drain, cover with fresh water and ½ teaspoon of the salt, and cook until tender (about 1 hour), adding more water if needed.

Measure the bulgur into a medium bowl. Bring the tomato juice to a boil and pour over the bulgur. Let stand.

In a large stovetop casserole or Dutch oven over medium heat, warm the oil. Sauté the onions and garlic until softened; reduce the heat to medium-low, stir in the celery and carrot, and cook for about 10 minutes. Add the bell pepper, jalapeño pepper, chili powder, lemon juice, cumin, basil, and the remaining ½ teaspoon salt; cook until the peppers are tender.

Reduce the heat to low and stir in the tomato, reserved bulgur, cooked beans, wine, and cayenne. Combine well and simmer for about 30 minutes. Top with the chopped cilantro and serve the yogurt on the side.

Serves 4 to 6.

Variations

Tempeh Chili. Sauté 1 ½ cups of tempeh (cut into ½-inch cubes) along with the onions and garlic.

Quick Vegetarian Chili. Substitute 2 cans (15 ounces each) red kidney beans, drained and rinsed, for the uncooked beans. Substitute 1 can (28 ounces) whole tomatoes, chopped, with juice, for the fresh tomato. Omit the wine. Prepare the bulgur and sautéed vegetables as above; then combine the other ingredients and simmer, uncovered, for 15 to 20 minutes.

Linguini with Broccoli, Cauliflower, and Mushrooms

This pasta dish, an adaptation of a much weightier version, provides a change from the usual tomato sauces. Purists may take issue with the use of farmer cheese, but the result is very good indeed.

1 cup farmer cheese
¼ cup grated Romano or Sapsago cheese
1 medium head cauliflower, cut into florets
1 medium bunch broccoli, cut into florets
2 tablespoons olive oil
6 cloves garlic, sliced thin
1 pound fresh mushrooms, sliced thick
¾ teaspoon salt
½ teaspoon cayenne pepper
1 pound linguini

Combine cheeses and set aside. In a large pot of boiling lightly salted water, cook the cauliflower and broccoli for about 5 minutes. Remove the vegetables with a slotted spoon, reserving the liquid for cooking the linguini.

In a large skillet, warm the oil. Lightly brown the garlic; stir in the mushrooms, salt, and cayenne; sauté for about 5 minutes.

Bring the vegetable liquid to a boil, adding enough water to make 4 quarts. Add the linguini, stir, and cook.

Meanwhile, stir the reserved broccoli and cauliflower into the garlic and mushrooms. Cover and continue cooking until the vegetables are just tender. Drain the pasta, stir into the vegetables, and heat thoroughly. Top with the reserved cheese mixture and serve immediately.

Serves 8.

INDEX

Specialty Cookbooks from The Crossing Press

Biscotti, Brownies, and Bars
By Terri Henry

$6.95 • Paper • ISBN 0-89594-901-6

Innovative Soy Cooking
By Trudi Burnham

$6.95 • Paper • ISBN 0-89594-962-8

Old World Breads
By Charel Scheele

$6.95 • Paper • ISBN 0-89594-902-4

Pestos! Cooking with Herb Pastes
By Dorothy Rankin

$8.95 • Paper • ISBN 0-89594-180-5

Quick Breads
By Howard Early and Glenda Morris

$6.95 • Paper • ISBN 0-89594-941-5

Salad Dressings
By Teresa H. Burns

$6.95 • Paper • ISBN 0-89594-895-8

Salsas!
By Andrea Chesman

$6.95 • Paper • ISBN 0-89594-178-3

Sauces for Pasta!
By K. Trabant with A. Chesman

$8.95 • Paper • ISBN 0-89594-403-0

Sun-Dried Tomatoes
By Andrea Chesman

$6.95 • Paper • ISBN 0-89594-900-8

Wholesome Cookies
By Jane Marsh Dieckmann

$6.95 • Paper • ISBN 0-89594-942-3

To receive a current catalog from The Crossing Press, please call toll-free, 800-777-1048.
Visit our Website on the Internet at: www.crossingpress.com